# Marketing Strategy in the Digital Age

# Marketing Strategy in the Digital Age

*Exploiting e-commerce in your business*

**Elizabeth Daniel, Hugh Wilson, Malcolm McDonald and John Ward**

FINANCIAL TIMES
Prentice Hall

Cranfield
UNIVERSITY
School of Management

PEARSON EDUCATION LIMITED

Head Office:
Edinburgh Gate
Harlow CM20 2JE
Tel: +44 (0)1279 623623
Fax: +44 (0)1279 431059

London Office:
128 Long Acre
London WC2E 9AN
Tel: +44 (0)20 7447 2000
Fax: +44 (0)20 7240 5771
Website: www.briefingzone.com

First published in Great Britain in 2001

ISBN 0 273 65479 9

*British Library Cataloguing in Publication Data*
A CIP catalogue record for this book can be obtained from the British Library.

10 9 8 7 6 5 4 3 2 1

Typeset by Monolith – www.monolith.uk.com
Printed and bound in Great Britain

*The Publishers' policy is to use paper manufactured from sustainable forests.*

# About the authors

**Dr Elizabeth Daniel** BSc, PhD, MBA is a Senior Research Fellow in the Information Systems Research Centre at Cranfield School of Management. Elizabeth has a first degree and PhD in Physics and an MBA from London Business School. She has spent over ten years in industry, starting her career as a Medical Engineer at GEC and more recently working in a leading strategy management consultancy, the LEK Partnership, where she undertook assignments across a number of industry sectors. Elizabeth undertakes teaching and research in the fields of e-business and new technologies in marketing. She has published a number of papers and management reports in these fields, including *Electronic Banking in Europe* (The Stationery Office, 1998) and *Profiting from eCRM* (Financial Times Prentice Hall, 2001, with Hugh Wilson).

**Dr Hugh Wilson** MA (Oxon), DipCompSci (Cantab), PhD is a Visiting Fellow and Director of the Centre for e-Marketing at Cranfield School of Management. After a mathematics degree at Oxford University and a postgraduate computer science degree at Cambridge University, he spent 13 years in the computing industry, before gaining a prize-winning PhD from Cranfield University on decision support systems for marketing planning. He has published amongst others, in the *British Journal of Management*, *Journal of Marketing Management* and *Journal of Marketing Strategy*. Books and management reports include *e-Marketing* (Financial Times Prentice Hall, 1999, with Malcolm McDonald).

**Professor Malcolm McDonald** MA (Oxon), MSc, PhD, FCIM, FRSA is Professor of Marketing Strategy and Deputy Director of Cranfield School of Management with special responsibility for e-Business. He is a graduate in English Language and Literature from Oxford University, in Business Studies from Bradford University Management Centre, and has a PhD from Cranfield University. He has extensive industrial experience, including a number of years as marketing director of Canada Dry. He is chairman of six companies and spends much of his time working with the operating boards of the world's biggest multinational companies. He has written 30 books, including the best seller *Marketing Plans: how to prepare them; how to use them* and many of his papers have been published. His current interests centre around the use of information technology in advanced marketing processes.

**Professor John Ward** MA, FCMA is Professor of Strategic Information Systems and Director of the Information Systems Research Centre at Cranfield School of Management. John's main areas of interest are the strategic uses of IS/IT, the integration of IS/IT strategies with business strategies, the development of organizational IS capabilities and the management of IS/IT investments. He has published papers on these and related topics in leading journals and is author/co-author of the books *Strategic Planning for Information Systems*, *The Principles of IS Management* and *The Essence of Information Systems*. Prior to joining Cranfield in 1984 he worked in industry for 15 years, the last three as Systems Development Manager at Kodak Limited. He acts as a consultant to a number of major international organizations. He has a degree in Natural Sciences from Cambridge, is a Fellow of the Chartered Institute of Management Accountants and is President of the UK Academy for Information Systems.

# Contents

# List of figures

# List of tables

# Cranfield School of Management Research Reports Series

*The Cranfield School of Management Research Reports* series is a major new initiative from Cranfield School of Management and Financial Times Prentice Hall.

The series combines the best in primary research from one of the world's foremost management schools with the traditional publishing and marketing skills of Financial Times Prentice Hall. The reports are designed to allow senior managers to apply the lessons from this research to their own organizations in order to promote best practice across a range of industries.

For further information on other titles in the series, please contact Financial Times Prentice Hall on +44 (0)1279 623333 or visit www.briefingzone.com.

## Editorial Board

Professor Alan Harrison, Professor of Operations and Logistics, Exel Research Fellow, Cranfield School of Management

Professor Malcolm McDonald, Professor of Marketing Strategy and Deputy Director, Cranfield School of Management

Gill Marshall, Director, Corporate Communications, Cranfield School of Management

Professor Sudi Sudarsanam, Professor of Finance and Corporate Control, Cranfield School of Management

Professor David Tranfield, Professor of Management, Director of Research and Deputy Director, Cranfield School of Management

Professor Shaun Tyson (Chairman), Professor of Human Resource Management and Head of the Strategic Human Resources Group, Cranfield School of Management

Professor Susan Vinnicombe, Professor of Organizational Behaviour and Diversity Management and Director of Graduate Research, Cranfield School of Management

# Acknowledgements

The authors of this report would like to acknowledge the contribution of a number of parties to the findings presented here.

The research project was sponsored by the following 17 organizations:

- Astra Zeneca
- Bacon & Woodrow
- Birmingham & Solihull TEC
- British Energy
- Cadbury Schweppes
- GlaxoWellcome
- Guardian Newspapers Ltd
- IBM
- Lease Plan
- Legal & General Assurance Society
- PHH Business Solutions
- Prudential
- Skandia Group
- SmithKline Beecham
- Thames Water
- West Sussex County Council
- Zurich Financial Services.

We would like to thank the sponsors of the project for their financial support and for their commitment of time in participating in the workshops that formed part of this study.

We would also like to thank the organizations in which case studies were undertaken. We would like to thank the managers involved within these organizations for their time and their insight and experience which we have endeavoured to distil in the findings of this report.

We would also like to acknowledge the following contributions to the material presented in this report.

- Dr Chris Hemingway, Research Fellow, Information Systems Research Centre, made a significant contribution to the material presented in this report, including the preparation of the case studies of Yelo Ltd and SmithKline Beecham.

- The ideas presented in the section discussing the measurement of e-commerce services were developed in collaboration with Professor Andy Neely and his colleagues from the Centre for Business Performance, Cranfield School of Management.

- Mr Peter Murray, Research Fellow, Information Systems Research Centre, collaborated in the case studies relating to Bacon & Woodrow, the card publisher and Cadbury Schweppes.

- Mr Phil Jones, formerly of Arjo Wiggins Fine Papers, researched and wrote the case study concerning e-procurement at Arjo Wiggins.

- Mr Joe Peppard, Senior Research Fellow, Information Systems Research Centre, helped in our review of existing research and literature.

# Executive summary

> The impact of the Internet economy is global, reaching both businesses and government. Business leaders worldwide recognize the strategic role that the Internet plays in their company's ability to survive and compete in the future. To be competitive in this new economy, companies need to harness the power of the Internet.
>
> John Chambers,
> President and CEO, Cisco Systems (2000)

*Companies must learn how they can make use of the Internet in their own businesses.*

## AN EFFECTIVE E-COMMERCE STRATEGY

Electronic commerce is one of the most discussed topics in business today. Its impact is already leading to the reshaping of customer and supplier relationships, the streamlining of business processes and, in some cases, even in the restructuring of whole industries. As stated by John Chambers, if companies wish to compete in this new era, they must learn how they can make use of the Internet in their own businesses, that is, they must develop an effective e-commerce strategy.

## A PRACTICAL PROCESS

This report aims to help organizations develop such an e-commerce strategy by presenting a practical process that they can follow in order to develop such a strategy. The process was developed as a result of a research programme undertaken by the Information Systems Research Centre and the Centre for e-Marketing at Cranfield School of Management, in collaboration with a number of leading companies and public-sector organizations.

## SIX STAGES

The suggested process consists of six stages that cover the entire strategy development process, from analysis, through change management issues to measurement and review. The six stages are:

- context and positioning

- market value analysis

- market vision

- prioritization and selection

- change management

- measurement and review.

## FRAMEWORKS

Each of the stages of the process is composed of a number of planning tools or frameworks. Organizations that have not yet commenced work on an e-commerce strategy should address each stage of the process. Organizations that already have a fledgling strategy can use particular stages of the process to augment the work they have already carried out. Even organizations that have a well-developed e-commerce strategy will find value in the tools in further exploring areas of their adopted strategy, for example, to see if the tools generate additional or alternative options to those already being explored.

## EXPERIMENTATION

For most companies it is not appropriate to use all of the tools suggested in each stage of the process: rather, the one or two tools in each stage that are of most use to the company should be adopted. Some element of experimentation with the tools will allow firms to find those that most powerfully describe their own situation.

## WELL-ESTABLISHED AND NEW TOOLS

The tools presented include both well-established planning tools and new ones that are suggested by the unique features of this domain. It may be expected that a field like e-commerce that is so new would require a brand new set of planning and analysis tools. However, in our research work we found that a number of well-established tools were still very useful in this new domain and hence they are included in the strategy development process. Where well-established tools are presented, their applicability to e-commerce is explicitly addressed.

## DIFFERENCES

The areas of this process differing most from traditional planning methods are:

- The initial, **context** stage, which must take account not just of the organization's objectives, but also of relevant aspects of its capabilities.

- The **market vision** stage. Many planning methods skip from an understanding of the industry's current structure to the issue of how the organization should position itself within that structure. The market vision stage adds the important step of predicting how the industry structure itself is likely to be changed as a result of e-commerce, quite independently of what position the planning organization takes towards e-commerce. The core tool of this stage is referred to as 'future market mapping'. Another new tool within this stage is 'value gap analysis'.

- The **change management** stage, in which the **applications portfolio**, a well-established tool in information systems (IS) strategy, is extended to examine how the portfolio of e-commerce applications should be managed.

## CASE STUDIES

Many aspects of the process were developed and refined through a series of case studies, covering organizations from different industry sectors and at different stages in their adoption of e-commerce. Where a case study exemplified a particular part of the strategy development process, it is discussed in the main text of this report. A fuller description of each of the case studies is included at the end of the report.

# 1

# Introduction

Electronic commerce is one of the most discussed topics in business today. Its impact is already leading to the reshaping of customer and supplier relationships, the streamlining of business processes and, in some cases, even in the restructuring of whole industries. Forecasts have estimated that the total value of e-commerce around the world will exceed $400 billion by 2002 (IDC, 2000). Although much of the media coverage of e-commerce concentrates on 'born to the web' companies such as Amazon.com or eBay, the benefits of e-commerce are also accruing to traditional businesses who are adopting this way of working. Research by the Boston Consulting Group (1999) in online retailing has shown that over 60 per cent of all e-commerce revenues in this sector are being earned by traditional companies that have launched websites to complement their existing business.

If companies wish to compete in this new era, they must learn how they can make use of the Internet in their own businesses, that is, they must develop an effective e-commerce strategy. This report aims to help organizations develop such an e-commerce strategy by presenting a process that they can follow in order to develop such a strategy. The process was developed as a result of a research programme undertaken by the Information Systems Research Centre and the Centre for e-Marketing at Cranfield School of Management, in collaboration with a number of leading companies and public-sector organizations.

*The benefits of e-commerce are also accruing to traditional businesses.*

Before developing the strategy development process, business managers from a range of industries were asking what key challenges they face when developing e-commerce services. The following four questions were commonly cited by those managers:

1.  **How can the value proposition of electronic commerce services be defined and used to drive customer and supplier acceptance?** Organizations developing electronic commerce services need to understand what elements of the service their customers or suppliers will value and use. Once this is established, services focused on these valued elements can be developed, and an associated communications strategy that increases uptake of the services can be adopted.

2.  **How can an electronic commerce strategy be defined and a business case built?** Many organizations are currently considering how best to develop an electronic commerce strategy and how this should relate to other existing strategic initiatives within the organization, such as the marketing strategy and the IS strategy. The cross-functional nature of electronic commerce requires that strategy formulation is

co-ordinated across the entire organization, which is currently a challenge to many organizations. In developing an electronic commerce strategy it is necessary to understand and be able to quantify the business benefits that may be obtained.

3. **How can business processes be aligned with electronic commerce services and the organizational implications be managed?** Companies are reaping the significant benefits from electronic commerce only if the services they develop are supported by fully aligned internal processes. Certain electronic commerce services effectively render the organization transparent to customers, and this requires managers to understand the implications of this transparency and to adapt working procedures accordingly.

4. **How can the effectiveness of electronic commerce developments be measured?** Organizations adopting e-commerce are keen to understand how they can measure the effectiveness of their services. If electronic commerce offers new ways of working, it might be expected that new metrics will be required to determine effectiveness.

The strategy process developed and presented in this report will allow business managers to answer each of these key questions for their own organization and hence develop an effective e-commerce strategy.

## 1.1 HOW TO USE THE STRATEGY DEVELOPMENT PROCESS

This report presents a number of tools that we have found during the research project to be useful to companies in their development of an e-commerce strategy. The tools are grouped into six stages that form a complete strategy development process. Companies that have not yet commenced work on an e-commerce strategy should address each stage of the process. Companies that already have a fledgling strategy can use particular stages of the process to augment the work they have already carried out. Even firms that have a well-developed e-commerce strategy will find value in the tools in further exploring areas of their adopted strategy, for example, to see if the tools generate additional or alternative options to those already being explored.

Each stage of the process contains a number of tools. For most companies it is not appropriate to use all of the tools in each stage: rather, the one or two tools in each stage that are of most use to the company should be adopted. Some element of experimentation with the tools will allow firms to find those that most powerfully describe their own situation.

The tools presented include both well-established planning tools and new ones that are suggested by the unique features of this domain. It may be expected that a field like e-commerce that is so new would require a brand new set of planning and analysis tools. However, in our research work we found that a number of well-established tools were still very useful in this new domain, and hence they are included in the strategy development process. Where well-established tools are presented, their applicability to e-commerce is explicitly addressed.

## 1.2 REPORT STRUCTURE

Following this introduction an overview of the e-commerce strategy development process is presented in section 2. Each of the six stages of the process is then covered in more depth in sections 3 to 8. Illustrations of the tools and frameworks suggested are drawn from the case studies, and a summary of each of the six case studies undertaken as part of the study is included (*see* Chapter 10).

*Where well-established tools are presented, their applicability to e-commerce is explicitly addressed.*

Finally, worksheets setting out the steps involved in some of the key strategy development tools have been developed to aid in their use in practice. These are presented at the end of the report (*see* page 117).

## 1.3 DEFINITION OF E-COMMERCE

Due to the rapid growth of e-commerce, no formal definitions have yet been widely agreed. It can be considered as: 'the buying and selling of information, products and services via computer networks' (Kalakota and Whinston, 1998). The term *electronic business* or *e-business*, which is now often used in place of *e-commerce*, is generally taken to cover the buying and selling described above and, in addition, supply chain and internal operational issues.

For the purposes of this report the term *electronic commerce* will be used to mean:

> the external relationships of an organization with both buyers and suppliers facilitated by computer networks. The internal processes and competencies necessary to support these external relationships will also be included.

Electronic business initiatives wholly inside the organization, such as the use of intranets for employee communication are therefore not included. The research addresses both business-to-business and business-to-consumer markets.

## 1.4  RESEARCH METHOD

The strategy development process presented in this report was developed in the following stages:

1.  Identification of frameworks/possible method components from previous research and literature

2.  Integration of these into an outline planning process

3.  Testing the outline process, or elements of it, by means of case studies in companies currently using e-commerce, conducted using a combination of interviews and workshops

4.  Adaptation of the outline process to fit lessons learned from the case studies.

Case studies were carried out in the following six organizations, some of which were also sponsors of the project:

- Cadbury Schweppes
- a greetings card publisher
- Yelo Ltd, a test and measurement equipment manufacturer
- Bacon & Woodrow
- Arjo Wiggins/RS Components
- SmithKline Beecham.

In larger organizations, the case studies undertaken were focused at the business unit/divisional level of the company, whilst in smaller organizations the whole company was considered. The current e-commerce strategy was explored, including how that strategy had been formulated. A particular project or initiative within the strategy was then examined in depth. The unit of analysis was therefore a project, but within its strategic context. All of the companies studied had some track record in e-commerce, whilst the projects studied ranged from fully operational systems to planned future developments.

Typically, the following approach was adopted for the case studies:

1. understand the e-commerce strategy of the business unit (and how this fits with the company e-commerce strategy)

2. understand where the project of interest fits with the strategy

3. explore the strategy development process the company uses, if any

4. see if the proposed strategy development process would have been useful to the company in defining or implementing its e-commerce strategy, by:

   a modelling part of the company's strategy using part of the process

   b examining the success of this strategy to date

   c comparing **a** and **b**.

5. see if the proposed strategy development process needs amending in any way to reconcile **4a** and **b** above.

Findings presented in this report are also drawn from a market-mapping workshop held with the following three financial services companies:

- Legal & General
- Skandia Group
- Zurich Financial Services.

# 2

# Overview of strategy development process

Electronic commerce is forecast to have a broad impact, affecting relations with customers and suppliers and even causing restructuring in whole industries. So it seems unlikely that one single model or framework could be sufficient to explain what an organization should do in this domain. The project has therefore identified a number of inter-related models, from the strategy, marketing and IS fields, as well as from more recent e-commerce literature, that can be used together to formulate an e-commerce strategy.

*We present here those frameworks which we have found of most value in working with companies using e-commerce.*

We present here those frameworks which we have found of most value in working with companies using e-commerce. The case studies tested these frameworks against existing e-commerce ventures in companies in order to see how well they explain their successes and difficulties. Examples of use of the frameworks drawn from the case studies are presented and discussed.

An overview of the proposed strategy development process is shown in Figure 2.1, and briefly described below.

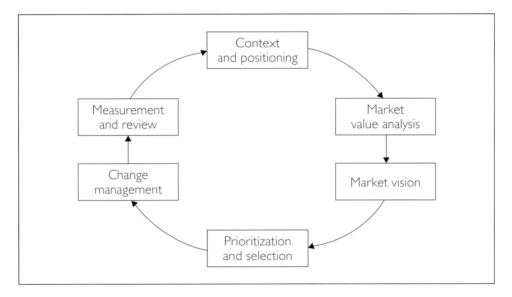

**FIGURE 2.1**

**Overview of e-commerce strategy development process**

- *Context and positioning*: To set the scene for the role of e-commerce, the process begins with a high-level examination of the industry and the organization's positioning within it.

- *Market value analysis*: Next, an understanding of the organization's place within the current industry structure is gained, including understanding of the value provided to customers.

- *Market vision*: Potential modifications to the current route to market are explored and evaluated in terms of their impact on customer value, in order to predict how the industry will change as a result of e-commerce.

- *Prioritization and selection*: The transition to a future vision cannot be accomplished at once, and the organization may not be able to take advantage of all the potential opportunities in the industry. In this stage, options are prioritized and selected.

- *Change management*: Chosen projects now need to be planned and implemented, including necessary changes to the way the organization conducts business as well as IT developments.

- *Measurement and review*: Finally, there is a need for the efficacy of e-commerce initiatives to be evaluated in order to inform future work.

The tools and frameworks suggested for each stage of the strategy development process are shown in Figure 2.2.

**FIGURE 2.2**

**Strategy development process tools**

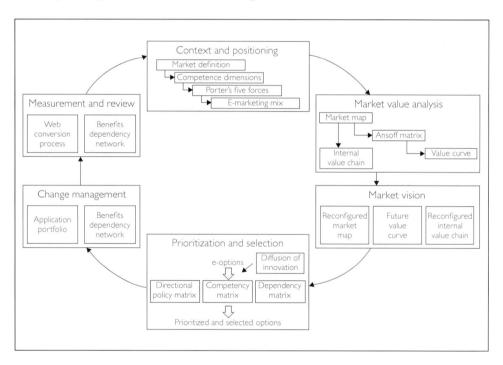

# 3

# Context and positioning

## 3.1 OVERVIEW

The purpose of this stage is to set the scene for the role of e-commerce, by a high-level examination of the industry and the organization's positioning within it. The stage is summarized in Figure 3.1.

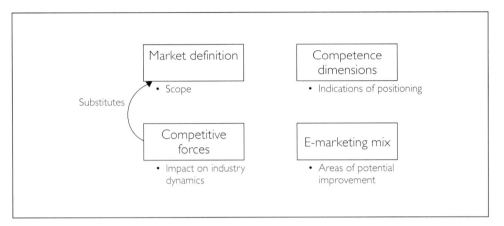

**FIGURE 3.1**
**Context and positioning**

First, a market definition is drafted for the market within which the organization operates. This will scope various analyses in the process, which relate to the market as a whole. The competitive forces analysis begins the process of assessing in broad terms how e-commerce might affect the market. Consideration of substitute products, in particular, might lead to a reconsideration of whether the market definition needs to be redrafted. The competence dimensions analysis complements this industry view by considering what the organization's strategic strengths and weaknesses are, and how these competencies might be built in the future. Finally, the e-marketing mix establishes a base-line of the organization's current maturity in its use of IT to support customer relationships.

*The e-marketing mix establishes a base-line of the organization's current maturity in its use of IT to support customer relationships.*

## 3.2 MARKET DEFINITION

As a first stage to any strategy development it is necessary to define the market that is to be addressed by the organization. As stated by McDonald and Dunbar (1998), the general rule for a market definition is that it should be described in terms of a customer need, in a way that covers all of the alternative products or services that customers regard as being capable of satisfying that need.

## Financial services market definition

A workshop was held with three financial service companies to explore the utility of the market-mapping technique, described in section 4.2 (page 30) of this report, in the formulation of e-commerce strategy. The first task undertaken in the workshop was to generate a market definition that could then form the basis of the market-mapping analysis. It was decided that the focus of the workshop would be the life, pensions and investments sector of financial services since this was a common interest of the companies present. Three separate market definitions were generated which were then brought together.

### *Group 1 led by Zurich Financial Services*

Group 1 believed that the market could be defined as 'asset accumulation for lifestyle protection'. The lifestyle events that protection is being sought for can be divided up into the three types shown in Table 3.1.

**TABLE 3.1**

**Financial services market definition**

| Lifestyle Events | Characteristics |
| --- | --- |
| I'll get old and have to retire | Certainty |
| I'll get sick or die early I'll need to pay for something | Uncertain and unpleasant |
| I'll need to buy things in the future/save for a big event | Uncertain and pleasant |

### *Group 2 led by Skandia Group*

A market definition of 'management of finances in order to meet current and future needs' was suggested. They felt that the market for financial management could be represented as shown in Figure 3.2.

In addition to the range of products within the timescale versus planning dimensions, companies provide advice as to which products are most suitable and also manage the invested funds with the intention of maximizing returns.

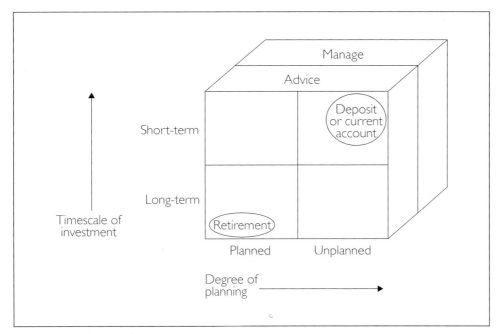

FIGURE 3.2

Financial services market definition

Short-term is 0–5 years and long-term is 5–15+ years

### Group 3 led by Legal & General

Group 3 suggested that the market could be defined by the four attributes or benefits that it provided to consumers:

1. Creation of wealth

   - Increase personal wealth
   - Wealth per family
   - Realizing dreams, avoiding nightmares

2. Income stream

   - Post-income: replacing income in future (sustaining quality of life)

3. Freedom of choice

   - Discretionary fund in later life

4. Control

   - Control over lifestyle by control over financial matters.

The above four market definitions illustrate a range of market definitions that could be adopted to describe the life, pensions and investment sector of the retail financial services sector. The important features of such definitions are that they are drafted in terms of customer needs, not products and that they cover all the alternative products and services that

*It is important that all relevant members of the organization are in agreement with the market definition.*

customers can utilize to satisfy that need. It is also important that all relevant members of the organization are in agreement with the market definition, since this will form the cornerstone of the organization's strategies, in e-commerce and in other areas of the business.

## 3.3 COMPETITIVE FORCES ANALYSIS

**Purpose:** To analyze the forces affecting competition in an industry.

**Description:** Five forces which affect industry competition are: the threat of new entrants, the threat of substitute products or services, the bargaining power of buyers and of suppliers and rivalry of existing competitors (*see* Figure 3.3). As part of business strategy development it is valuable to assess the impacts of each force (high, medium or low for instance) and then to describe the nature of the impact where it is high, in order to identify ways of counteracting that force.

**FIGURE 3.3**

**Competitive forces in an industry**

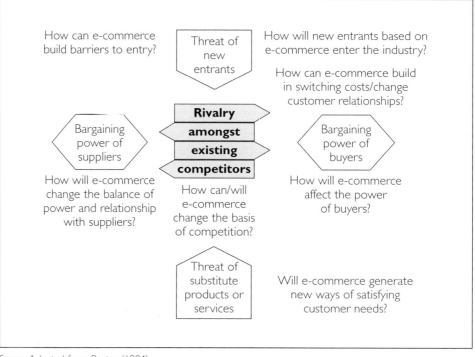

*Source:* Adapted from Porter (1984).

**Adapting the tool to e-commerce:** Figure 3.4 summarizes some of the key implications of this analysis, and gives examples of ways in which IT investments can influence the situation. All of these are of relevance to e-commerce. New entrants in the form of intermediaries between existing competitors and their customers, while not a new phenomenon, are particularly important in the e-commerce context, as the information-processing advantages of the medium are well suited to intermediaries, while the fast-moving nature of the field makes new entrants difficult to predict. Other impacts on the industry structure arise from 'e-clubs' which increase the buying leverage of groups of people with similar interests, and switch industries towards a different way of trading, such as auctions rather than fixed pricing. Potential changes to industry structure identified using this tool are explored in more detail in the market vision stage.

**FIGURE 3.4**
**Competitive forces and IS/IT**

| Impact of competitive forces and potential IS/IT opportunities | | |
| --- | --- | --- |
| *Key force impacting the industry* | *Business implications* | *Potential IS/IT effects* |
| Threat of new entrants | Additional capacity <br><br> Reduced prices <br><br> New basis for competition | Provide entry barriers/reduce access by: <br> • exploiting existing economies of scale <br> • differentiate products/services <br> • control distribution channels <br> • segment markets |
| Buyer power high | Forces prices down <br><br> Demand higher quality | Differentiate products/services and improve price/performance |
| | Require service flexibility | Increase switching costs of buyers |
| | Encourage competition | Facilitate buyer product selection |
| Supplier power high | Raises prices/costs | Supplier sourcing systems |
| | Reduced quality of supply | Extended quality control into suppliers |
| | Reduced availability | Forward planning with supplier |
| Substitute products threatened | Limits potential market and profit <br><br> Price ceilings | Improve price/performance <br><br> Redefine products and services to increase value <br><br> Redefine market segments |
| Intense competition from rivals | Price competition <br><br> Product development <br><br> Distribution and service critical <br><br> Customer loyalty required | Improve price/performance <br><br> Differentiate products and services in distribution channel and to consumer <br><br> Get closer to the end consumer – understand the requirements |

*Source:* Adapted from Cash (1988).

## 3.4 DIMENSIONS OF COMPETENCE

**Purpose:** To balance the external view of competitive forces analysis with an internal view which considers what aspects of business performance the organization has the skills to excel in as a basis for achieving market leadership.

**Description:** This tool suggests that there are three paths to market leadership (*see* Figure 3.5):

- *'Operational excellence'*: enabling products and services to be obtained reliably, easily and cost effectively by customers, implying a focus on business processes to outperform others delivering both low costs and consistent quality of customer satisfaction. E.g., Dell, Wal-Mart, Federal Express.

**FIGURE 3.5**

**Dimensions of competence**

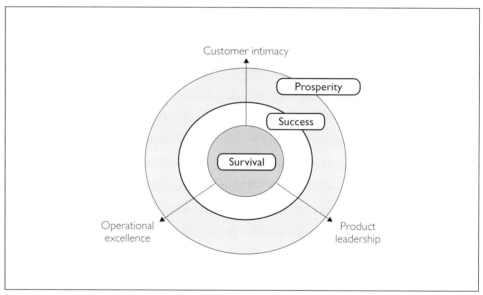

*Source:* Adapted from Treacy and Wiersema (1993).

- *'Customer intimacy'*: targeting markets precisely and tailoring products and services to the needs of particular customer groups, exceeding expectations and building loyalty. E.g., RS Components (UK), Home Depot (US).

- *'Product leadership'*: continuing product innovation that meets customers' needs. This implies not only creativity in developing new products and enhancing existing ones, but also astute market knowledge to ensure they sell. Johnson and Johnson, for example, pioneered the introduction of disposable contact lenses.

Excellence in one of these 'dimensions of competence', matched by a reasonable degree of performance on the others (i.e., not falling below the 'success' line in the figure), can lead to a strong competitive position. Understanding one's skills in existing product-markets can help to position one's offering in new ones. Equally, the analysis may suggest that a new business environment requires the development of new competencies.

**Adapting the tool to e-commerce:** Figure 3.6 suggests some key questions organizations can ask in relation to how e-commerce might affect its strategy in each of these dimensions.

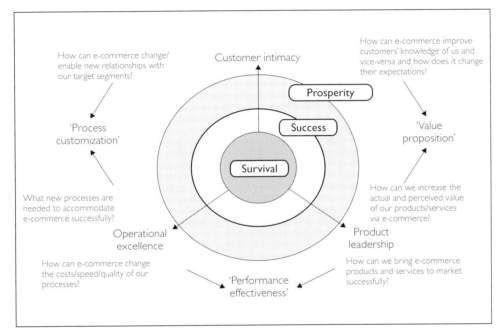

**FIGURE 3.6**

**The impact of e-commerce on the dimensions of competence**

*Source*: Adapted from Treacy and Wiersema (1993).

## 3.5 SERVING DISTRIBUTORS AT SCHWEPPES SA, SPAIN

Schweppes SA, in Spain is part of the Cadbury Schweppes Group of companies. It sells a range of branded soft drinks to the food or grocery market and the catering market. The catering market, termed HORECA in Spain, is made up of a large number of small operations of different types, such as hotels, restaurants, bars, clubs and sports clubs. Schweppes addresses the HORECA by use of two different types of distributor, direct and indirect. Direct distributors receive and despatch orders taken by Schweppes salesmen who visit customer premises. Indirect distributors employ their own sales force to deal with customers.

Schweppes SA have developed an Internet-based system to allow them to exchange information with their indirect distributors. The intention of this system is to improve their service to these distributors and also gaining and improved understanding of the end customer, that is the bar, disco or club who stocks Schweppes products.

Figure 3.7 illustrates the competitive position of Schweppes SA with respect to the three dimensions of business competence.

**FIGURE 3.7**

**Schweppes SA: dimensions of competence**

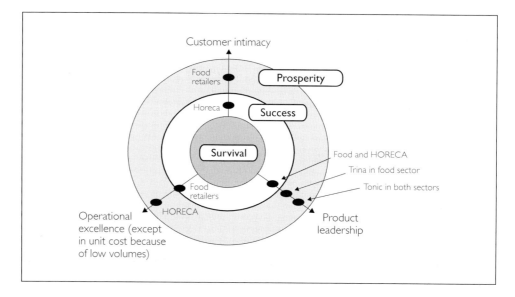

### Product leadership

Product innovation in the soft drinks market is almost impossible and so product leadership in this market is determined by brand strength. Schweppes SA have a leading position in tonic and in their fruit-based Trina brand – but in other products they compete with other players, some of whom are very powerful, such as Coke. Schweppes products currently tend to be premium priced in the categories they operate in and they intend to continue high levels of spending on brand advertising in order to be able to maintain these premium price levels.

### Operational excellence

Schweppes believe that operationally they perform better than others in the market in all areas apart from the unit cost of their products. Their unit costs tend to be high due to the relatively low volumes they currently produce and an increase in sales volume would reduce this key parameter.

*Schweppes SA have developed an Internet-based system to allow them to exchange information with their indirect distributors.*

## Customer intimacy

Schweppes believe they currently perform well relative to competitors with respect to the relationship with their customers in the food or grocery sector. However, due to the very large number of customers in the HORECA market, it is much more difficult for them to understand these customers and build such a close relationship. They therefore wish to improve their understanding and relationship with this highly competitive channel.

## Business drivers

Given the above analysis, the company's current key business drivers are:

- to grow volume whilst maintaining high margins in order to reduce unit costs

- invest in brand building to be able to maintain premium prices

- respond to the highly competitive nature of the HORECA market by improving customer intimacy.

Overall Schweppes SA wish to continue and improve prosperity in a profitable sector of the marketplace. Any e-commerce strategy or project should therefore address one or all of the three key drivers stated above. The distributors' system has a number of objectives that address the key drivers. These are:

- To gain knowledge of the end-customers of their indirect distributors in the HORECA market. This will allow improved marketing to these customers and, hence, will increase sales volumes.

- To improve the relationship with these indirect distributors to ensure they stay working with Schweppes rather than distributing competitors' products:

  - by helping them better understand and serve their customers

  - make it easier to do business with Schweppes.

## 3.6 THE E-MARKETING MIX

**Purpose:** To assess how well the organization is currently using IT to support customer communications, whether through the Internet or other channels. Using the tool also typically leads to ideas as to how IT-enabled channels can further enhance customer relationships, whose value to the customer can then be assessed by the value curve technique (described within the market value analysis stage).

**Description:** The model (*see* Figure 3.8) postulates that there are six ways in which IT can add value at the customer interface: (a) *integration* or sharing of customer data across the various channels used to reach them, leading to more efficient service; (b) *interactivity* in the communication with the customer, so their needs can be fully understood and responded to; (c) *independence of location*, enabling the supplier to serve efficiently customers who may be widely distributed geographically; (d) *individualization* of the product/service, or of marketing communications; (e) providing *intelligence* about customer needs, and hence informing the company's marketing strategy; and, finally, (f) *industry restructuring*, by enabling an industry player to sell directly rather than go through intermediaries, or alternatively to set up a new intermediary providing added value through information.

**FIGURE 3.8**

**The e-marketing mix**

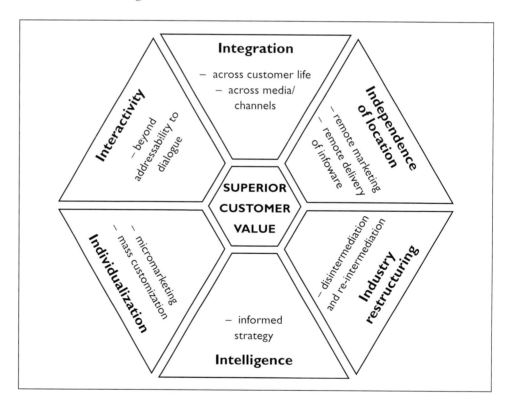

By plotting an organization's current position against each of these six dimensions, assigning values of, say, 'high', 'medium' and 'low' to how well it uses IT to achieve these aims, a picture can be built up of where the organization is currently strong and where it is relatively weak.

**Adapting the model to e-commerce:** While the tool applies equally to other channels such as telemarketing and direct mail, it works well in the e-commerce context. What the model does not of itself do is specify which of a number of potential improvements would actually add customer value. It can, though, form a bridge between 'technical speak' and 'marketing speak', generating ideas which can be tested by the value curve technique described in the market value analysis section.

# 4

# Market value analysis

## 4.1 OVERVIEW

The purpose of this stage is to gain an understanding of the organization's place within the current industry structure, including an understanding of the value provided to customers. This is used in the following, market vision stage to predict how the market structure and value proposition might be modified due to e-commerce. The stage is summarized in Figure 4.1.

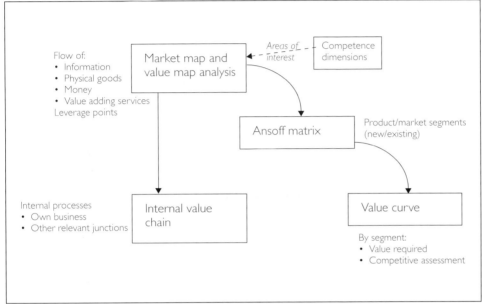

FIGURE 4.1
**Market value analysis stage**

*The purpose of market value analysis is to gain an understanding of the organization's place within the current industry structure.*

First a *market map* or *external value chain* is developed showing the chain, or more generally the network, from producers to consumers within the industry. This is annotated to show the flow not just of physical goods but also of information and money between elements of the chain. Where one element provides value-adding services to another, this is also shown. The map can also be annotated with the leverage points where purchase decisions are made. For example, within retail financial services independent financial advisers form a leverage point, as many consumers accept their recommended product supplier. They are mostly paid via commission from product providers. They combine information from product providers with information from the consumer, adding value through the provision of advice.

Which areas of the map are developed in most detail may depend on the competence analysis conducted earlier. For example, a need to improve operational excellence might suggest thorough mapping back through the supply chain as well as forwards to the customer, while a focus on customer intimacy might suggest a concentration on thorough mapping forwards towards the consumer. One extension that has been made to market mapping is *value gap analysis*, which examine adjacent organizations in the chain from producer to consumer, with a view to identifying ways in which the value exchange can be enhanced throughout the entire sales process by the use of e-commerce.

An *internal value chain analysis* can then be conducted on the organization's own business, and on other relevant parts of the chain (such as immediate customers), to show how they are organized to provide value to the next element in the chain to the consumer.

Another use of the market map is as a starting-point for segmentation. Any leverage points are segmented into groups with similar needs. These segments can be shown on an *Ansoff matrix*, which also shows the different product groups that are, or might be, provided to these segments. The *value curve* then shows the buying criteria of each segment, and how existing competitors meet these criteria.

## 4.2 MARKET MAPPING AND EXTERNAL VALUE CHAIN ANALYSIS[1]

**Purpose:** To represent the way in which the various organizations within an industry play a role in the product or service that is eventually delivered to the customer.

**Description:** Value chain analysis typically shows the value contributed by each organization in an industry in the production and delivery of goods or services to customers. A generic external value chain is shown in Figure 4.2.

External value chain analysis has long been a valuable tool in the development of information systems strategies. Having described the main components of the organization in terms of value-adding stages, the existing industry structure of the organizations involved can be overlaid. The role of information flows and exchanges amongst the organizations can be described, to identify those which have the greatest impact on industry performance at each stage and overall. All of these key information exchanges can be an opportunity for e-commerce investments, either by the firm itself or its competitors or trading partners. An example of value chain analysis in the pharmaceutical market, illustrating the critical information flows is shown in Figure 4.3.

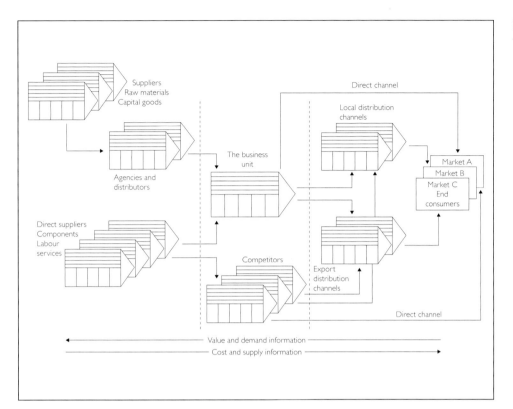

**FIGURE 4.2**
**The external value chain**

*Source:* Reproduced with permission from *Strategic Planning for Information Systems,* Ward and Griffiths, 1996.

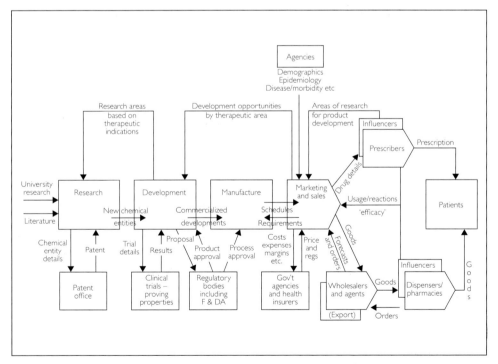

**FIGURE 4.3**
**Value chain for a pharmaceutical company**

*Source:* Reproduced with permission from *Strategic Planning for Information Systems,* Ward and Griffiths, 1996.

A market map is a similar concept to value chain analysis in that it shows how a market or industry works, by showing how goods and services flow from producers through intermediaries to the end customer. However, rather than show the value added by each participant in the chain, the market map shows the volume and value of products passing along each section of the chain. A market map shows the flow of all products in a market, thus it includes the route to market of competitors' products. It also includes organizations that are not directly involved with the production and distribution of the products, but who play an important part in the influencing the purchasing decision at each stage of the chain. These points in the market map where purchasing decisions are made are termed *leverage points* and recognition and understanding of these leverage points are important for the players in that market.

Figure 4.4 shows a market map for the agricultural fertilizer market. It can be seen that in addition to the manufacturers and end-user farmers, there are a number of important experts that influence the fertilizers bought, such as consultants and the specialist press. The role of these experts may become an increasingly important service when the impact of e-commerce on this industry or market is considered. For example, they may establish an online advisory or portal service which would have the advantage of being independent of any single manufacturer.

**FIGURE 4.4**

**Agricultural fertilizer market map**

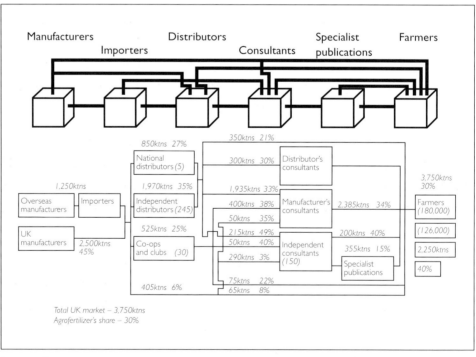

Source: McDonald and Dunbar (1998).

**Adapting the tools to e-commerce:** It was found during the research project that a combination of both the value chain and market mapping approaches should be adopted to provide the most informative starting point for e-commerce strategy development. A map should be developed that shows the following three flows:

- *Information flows*: both information on demand flowing from right to left, and information on supply and cost flowing from left to right

- *Physical flows*: of goods and services

- *Monetary flows*: showing where value is added and where value is appropriated.

A two-stage process should be adopted for this analysis. A composite map of the current market should be drawn and then a map showing how e-commerce is likely to impact the current map should be drawn. Developing a map of the future market is discussed in section 5.2 (page 44) of this report.

*A workshop was held with three financial services companies in order to test the utility of the market-mapping technique.*

## 4.3 FINANCIAL SERVICES CURRENT MARKET MAPPING

As discussed earlier in this report, a workshop was held with three financial services companies in order to test the utility of the market-mapping technique for e-commerce strategy development. The participants, who focused their analysis on the long-term personal investment market, developed the map of the current market shown in Figure 4.5.

As can be seen from Figure 4.5, there are a significant number of stages in this market and a number of different types of player at each stage. Ideally, the map should be developed further to show the interrelationships between the players and the volume or value of business passing along each branch.

The leverage points are marked with an arrow with the estimated percentage of the total consumer business that is decided at that point shown by the arrow. This analysis clearly shows that agents are responsible for the majority (70 per cent) of purchasing decisions in this market. Table 4.1 shows what happens if this 70 per cent is split according to the type of agent.

**FIGURE 4.5**

**Long-term personal
investment: current market**

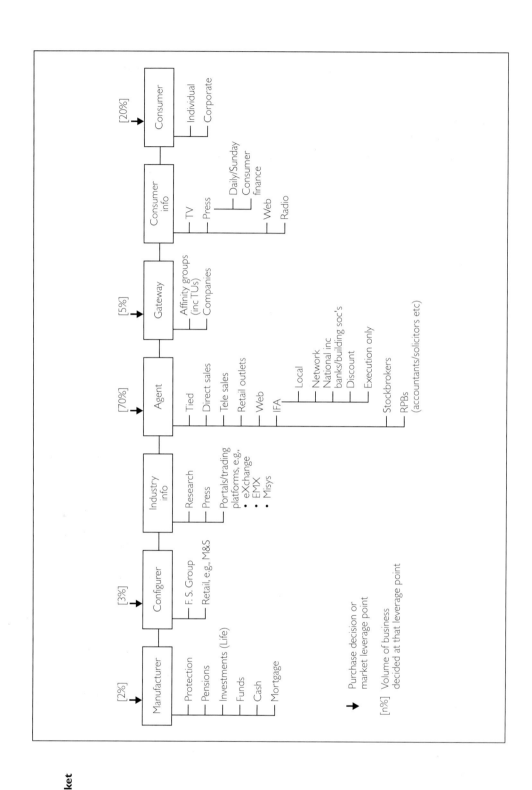

| Type of agent | Volume of agent-influenced sales |
|---|---|
| Independent financial adviser (IFA) | 40% |
| Tied agents, direct tele-sales and retail outlets | 25% |
| Stockbrokers and other registered professional bodies | 5% |
| Total | 70% |

**TABLE 4.1**

**Sales of long-term financial services products by agents**

## 4.4 VALUE GAP ANALYSIS

**Purpose:** To examine the value provided by suppliers and the value required by customers at each stage of the buying process.

**Description:** Figure 4.6 illustrates that there are a number of stages involved in the buying of a product or service. The supplier perspective is shown in the left-hand column and the traditional view of the buyer is shown in the right-hand column. The central column shows how we suggest these two separate views should be reconciled in the online world.

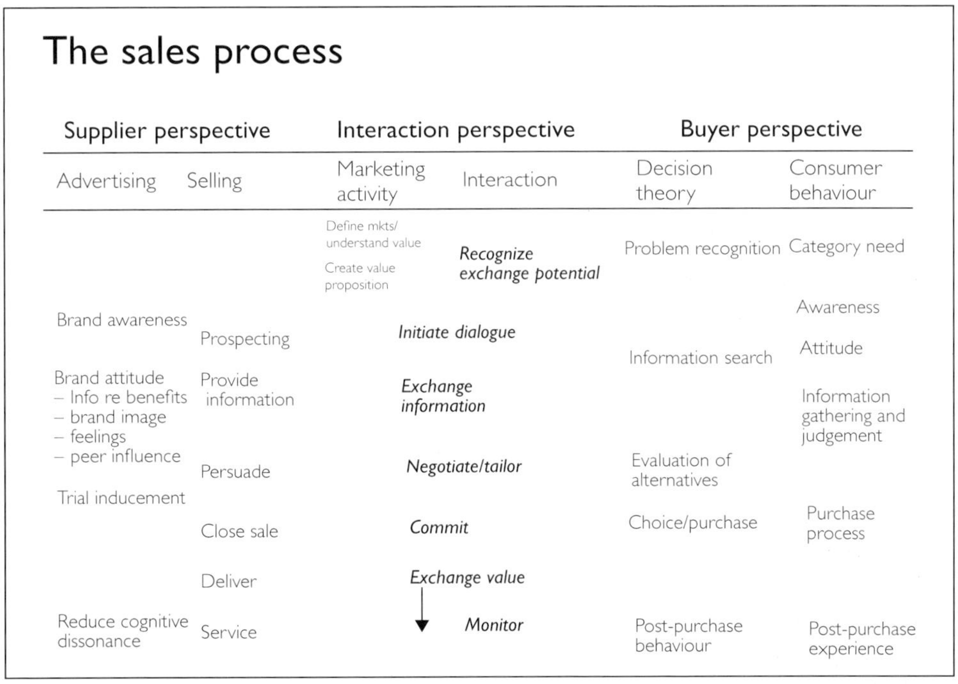

**FIGURE 4.6**

**Customer buying process**

Rather than 'problem recognition' on the part of the buyer, we label the first stage *recognize exchange potential* – a mutual recognition of the potential for an exchange of value which is beneficial to both parties. Rather than prospecting, we use the term *initiate dialogue*, to emphasize that the dialogue may be initiated by either party. Rather than just the seller providing information, the parties *exchange information* about the buyer's needs as well as the seller's offerings. Persuasion may be involved, but more generally the parties *negotiate and tailor* what will be provided by the seller, and what value (typically though not exclusively monetary) the buyer will provide in return. Closing the sale is better viewed as a *commit* step from both parties. The post-sales service is really a crucial part of the *exchange of value* which takes place, as the service surround becomes increasingly important in differentiating similar basic products. Finally, both parties will wish to *monitor* the value they have given and what they have received. This stage of after-sales contact is a very important stage in the buying process. Many companies still think of this contact in terms of warranties on technical products, but after-sales contact can be used in other markets to keep in touch with the customer and hence be well-placed if they wish to make an additional or replacement purchase of the product in question.

**Adapting the tool for e-commerce:** Although much emphasis of e-commerce is directed at the development of systems to allow customers to place orders and pay for goods online, companies developing e-commerce strategies should ensure they address all of the stages shown in Figure 4.6. Table 4.2 sets out how each stage of the buying process can be considered according to the value currently provided by the seller compared to the value required by the customer. A difference between these two indicates there is a value gap. The development of e-commerce services to address each of these value gaps should be investigated. This tool can not only be used to explore the potential for e-commerce between the end-consumer and their supplier, but between any pair of adjacent players in the value chain.

**TABLE 4.2**

**Value gap analysis**

| Stage of the buying process | Value provided by seller | Value gap/ e-commerce opportunities | Value required by customer |
|---|---|---|---|
| Recognize exchange potential | | | |
| Initiate dialogue | | | |
| Exchange information | | | |
| Negotiate/tailor | | | |
| Commit | | | |
| Exchange of value | | | |
| Monitor post-purchase relationship | | | |

## 4.5 INTERNAL VALUE CHAIN ANALYSIS

**Purpose:** To optimize the internal processes and information flows of the organization by analyzing how it adds value to its inputs. In particular, the analysis can help to ensure that IT investments enable the flow of key information through the business to optimize its overall performance, rather than simply fitting the existing organizational structure.

**Description:** The value chain approach, Figure 4.7, distinguishes *primary activities* – those which enable it to fulfil its role in the industry value chain by adding value – from *support activities* – which are necessary to control and develop the business over time. Porter classified the primary activities into five groupings: inbound logistics, operations, outbound logistics, sales and marketing and services. This structuring of the activities most easily fits a manufacturing company, but using the same logic of obtaining resources, transforming them, selling the result and delivering it, value chains can be drawn for any business.

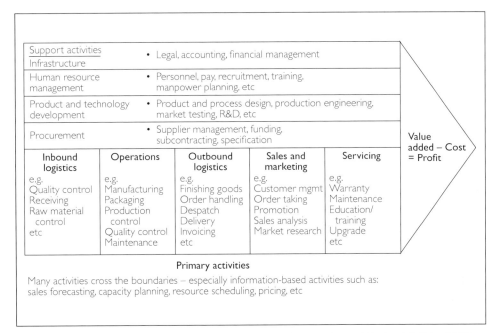

**FIGURE 4.7**

**The internal value chain**

*Source*: Reproduced with permission from *Strategic Planning for Information Systems*, Ward and Griffiths (1996).

**Adapting the tool to e-commerce:** In cases where external e-commerce changes trading relationships, internal processes and systems will also have to change to enable the new business model to operate efficiently. An understanding of the current internal value chain will aid in its redesign for a future scenario. One complication is that e-commerce often enables a different ordering of Porter's primary activities, where for example the product is ordered to a custom specification before it is manufactured. This has long been apparent in many service industries such as consultancies. In such cases the customer is actively involved in the process as well as being the recipient of the output and the value chain may look more like Figure 4.8.

**FIGURE 4.8**

**An alternative organization of internal activities**

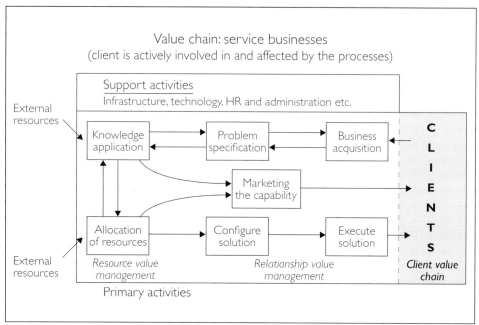

*Source*: Adapted from Satbell and Fjeldstad (1998).

Satbell and Fjeldstad (1998) have also considered the linear value chain of Porter too limited in certain situations and have suggested two alternative models of value creation: the value shop and the value network. The value shop is an organization that adds value by application of expertise to problem situations in a 'one-off' manner because each problem has some different characteristics from previous ones. Examples are medical diagnosis, geophysical surveys and so on. In contrast to the value chain the value shop is characterized by heavy dependence on expertise, significant use of hi-tech aids, iteration, and learning as a formal activity to improve the problem-solving capability of the organization. The value network is an organization that adds value by networking other organizations or individuals together. The obvious example is a telecommunications company, but banks would fall into this category since they essentially link lenders and borrowers. They have a heavy dependence on their infrastructure and in the private sector they have to collaborate with their competitors.

Confusion and value reduction can occur when an organization mistakes which kind of value organization it is. For example, a hospital (value shop) might try to run itself as a value chain (production line) and attempt to 'process' its patients in a highly uniform manner, setting success criteria which are concerned with throughput targets instead of, for example, targets related to health care and quality of life.

## 4.6 VALUE CURVE[2]

**Purpose:** To summarize the value being offered to customers by competitors within an industry. This can form the basis for identifying weaknesses that need to be addressed, as well as more pro-actively defining a positioning which will enhance the value delivered. It can be used when considering an e-commerce investment to model what customer value will result.

**Description:** Figure 4.9 illustrates a value curve for a book market. In this case, a company considering a net channel is comparing this channel with others available to its customers, though such a diagram can as readily be drawn to compare a number of competitors using the same channel. The criteria used should be those which matter to the customer, so ideally should be based on market research. Note that the analysis will vary per segment, so the book market would need a number of different value curves corresponding to such different needs as browsing for a present or ordering a business book from the workplace.

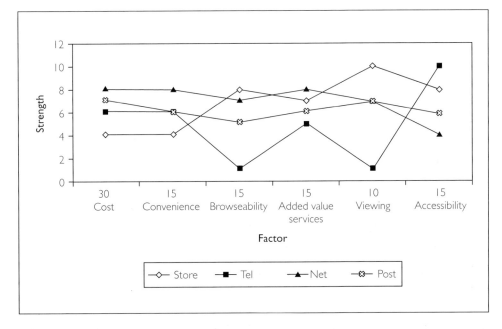

**FIGURE 4.9**

**Value curve for a book market**

**Adapting the tool to e-commerce:** An e-commerce market for one's particular product may not yet exist, so making market research difficult.

However, one can study the ways in which customer needs are currently being met, and estimate from those what the customers' buying criteria are. In addition, e-commerce may offer an opportunity to provide added-value services that meet needs not previously met by offline equivalents. Modelling these requires creativity, as although the needs for these services will have already existed, market research focused narrowly on the core product will not necessarily reveal the relevant buying criteria. Anticipating customer needs is an old problem, but one felt acutely by those in the fast-moving e-commerce field.

## NOTES

1  The external value chain approach is described in Porter (1984); Rayport and Svoikla (1995); and Ward (2000). We have combined it with the market-mapping approach described by McDonald and Dunbar (1998).

2  Kim and Mauborgne (1999). The approach is almost identical to the channel matrix proposed by McDonald and Wilson (1999a), except that they propose a stacked bar chart display of the same information.

# 5

# Market vision

---

## 5.1 OVERVIEW

In this stage, potential modifications to the current route to market are explored and evaluated in terms of their impact on customer value, in order to predict how the industry will change as a result of e-commerce. The stage is summarized in Figure 5.1.

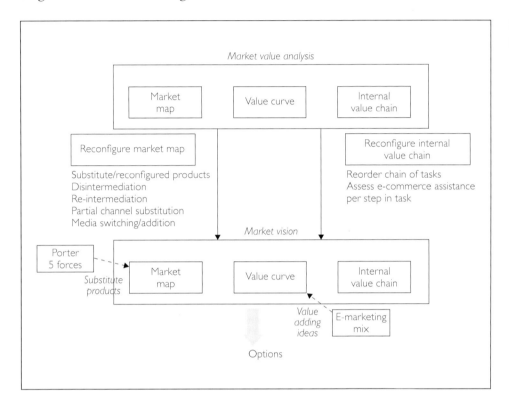

**FIGURE 5.1**
**Market vision stage**

The essence of this stage is to revisit the market map, value curve and internal value chain developed in the previous stage, and consider in what ways they might be affected by e-commerce. *Reconfigure market map* involves examining the current market map, and redrawing it to take account of various possible effects of e-commerce. *Reconfigure internal value chain* similarly re-examines the internal value chain, to see whether the introduction of e-commerce would suggest any changes to the way in which the organization conducts business. In both cases, the acid test as to whether a possible modification is accepted is whether the *value curve* for the consumer is improved thereby.

*Potential modifications to the current route to market are explored and evaluated in terms of their impact on customer value.*

The *competitive analysis* exercise conducted earlier using Porter's five forces may be relevant in reconfiguring the market map, for example through suggesting substitute products. Areas where the organization could improve in the *e-marketing mix* may suggest value-adding ideas – for example, greater individualization through online product specification on the Web – whose value can again be assessed by re-examining the value curve that would result.

The resulting vision of how the industry will change as a result of e-commerce presents the organization with choices as to how to position itself in the anticipated future industry structure, and how to manage the transition period. The resulting list of options can be prioritized in the stage that follows.

## 5.2 RECONFIGURED MARKET MAP

There are five main ways in which the market map can be reconfigured:

1. *Substitute/reconfigured products:* An electronic channel may enable the underlying customer need to be satisfied in a different way ('substitute products'). For example, e-mail can substitute for physical post, providing a threat to paper manufacturers, stationers and post offices. Or customer needs may be bundled into different product configurations ('reconfigured products'). The newspaper, for example, is a bundled product providing job advertisements, weather information, news, consumer-to-consumer advertisements and so on. It is now competing with web services which in some cases simply provide one of these components – such as consumer auction sites – or in others, combine some aspect of the value provided by newspapers with other types of value. For example, a portal such as Yahoo meets some of these needs, such as the day's news, and acts as a gateway to others, such as weather and auction sites, while also satisfying further needs not covered by the newspaper through the ability to search the Web. It can be seen that reconfigured products add complexity to the process, as two market maps from different industries may 'collide' and need to be considered together.

2. *Disintermediation:* As with other IT-enabled channels such as call centres, e-commerce can enable a link to be removed from the market map, by removing intermediaries whose primary function of information transfer can be more effectively performed using the Internet. Examples are telephone and Internet banking; direct purchase from clothes manufacturers via websites; and the bypassing of sales agents and distributors by some consumer goods manufacturers who are selling direct to retailers.

3. *Re-intermediation:* In some cases, a previous intermediary is replaced by an new online intermediary, rather than bypassed. Online sites which automatically search for the cheapest car insurance are competing with telephone-based brokers, which in turn caused the demise of the AA's high-street shops. General Electric's TPN Register provides an online marketplace between suppliers on the one hand, and GE and its partners on the other.

Predicting what re-intermediation will occur is difficult, as the possibilities are numerous. Will a given relationship – say, between CTN (confectioners, tobacconists and newsagents) stores and their suppliers – be a direct one? If so, will the shops buy from a range of suppliers' websites, or will the suppliers respond to tender requests on shop websites? Or will there be a new intermediary acting as a marketplace between the two? As shown in Figure 5.2, possibilities can be placed in an approximate order, from suppliers' website (such as Japan Airlines, which puts out open invitations to tender to suppliers), at one extreme, to vendor's website (such as Harvard Business Review, which provides an online version at a cost) at the other.

Neutral marketplaces are midway between the two. An example is an auction site, which is tied neither to the buyer nor the seller. Somewhat closer to the vendors are intermediaries such as Auto-by-Tel, which passes on leads to a local dealer. A more buyer-oriented intermediary is TPN Register, which we discussed earlier: set up by a consortium of buyers, it acts to ensure that they gain low prices through economies of scale.

> *Will the shops buy from a range of suppliers' websites, or will the suppliers respond to tender requests on shop websites?*

| | | |
|---|---|---|
| • Vendor-controlled | Vendor website | *Ernst & Young, HBR* |
| • Vendor-oriented | Vendor-run community<br>Consortium distributor<br>Vendor's agent<br>Lead generator<br>Audience broker | *Cambridge Information Net<br>thetrainline<br>Tesco financial services<br>Auto-By-Tel<br>DoubleClick* |
| • Neutral | Market maker<br>Shop<br>Mall | *eBay, FastParts, priceline<br>RS Components, Blackwell's<br>msn.com* |
| • Buyer-oriented | Purchaser's agent<br>Purchasing aggregator | *comparenet<br>TPN Register* |
| • Buyer-controlled | Buyer website | *Japan Airlines* |

**FIGURE 5.2**
**Types of intermediaries**

Which of these possibilities becomes the dominant trading mechanism in a given relationship depends on the number of vendors and buyers, and the relative power of suppliers and buyers. Where there are few buyers and many suppliers, or buyer power is great, the market will tend towards either individual buyer websites or buyer-oriented intermediaries, such as those being set up by car manufacturers. Conversely, a small number of suppliers selling to large numbers of customers will have the power to control the market through their own websites or through supplier-oriented consortia. Large numbers of both suppliers and buyers will tend to use a neutral marketplace to reduce the search costs of both parties, though a supplier with a particularly strong offering, such as *Harvard Business Review*, may choose not to participate in such marketplaces.

4. *Partial channel substitution:* This forms a halfway house towards disintermediation. In some cases, an intermediary's role may be reduced but not eliminated, through some of their value being provided remotely by the supplier to the intermediary's customer. Websites such as those of car manufacturers may build a brand and provide customer information while pointing customers to traditional outlets for actual purchase.

5. *Media switching/addition:* Finally, the links in the chain may remain the same, but communication between them may be partially or fully switched to the Internet from the previous mechanisms. Examples are Dell's addition of the Internet to its other means of communicating with customers, and RS Components, who have similarly added a web channel to its dominant telephone sales model, while still selling to the same customers.

## Reconfiguring the map

To reconfigure the market map, therefore, one needs to consider the potential effect of each of these five broad changes in turn. In each case, one needs to:

a   Sketch the effect of the change on the market map

b   Sketch the resulting effect on the customer's value curve (for each segment) c   If the effect is positive for some segments, incorporate the transformation in a revised market map.

Whether the effect on the value curve is regarded as positive depends on the organization's positioning within the relevant market. In terms of Michael Porter's three generic strategies this will imply:

* For *low-cost strategies*, an approximate parity needs to be ensured on non-price criteria, while beating the competition on price.

* For *differentiation strategies*, excellence needs to be ensured on one or more value-related criteria, while ensuring approximate parity on others.

* For *niche strategies*, strength needs to be high on criteria important to the target niches.

Table 5.1 contains some additional questions for disintermediation, partial channel substitution and media switching/addition.

| | |
|---|---|
| Disintermediation | Does the removal of an intermediary improve physical flows? |
| | If so, can information flows or other value-adding services provided by the intermediary be as effectively handled by others in the chain? |
| | Can the flow improvements be translated into an enhanced value curve? |
| Partial channel substitution | Does the addition of an Internet communication channel improve information flows (e.g., cheaper communication with customer)? |
| | Can relationship with intermediary be redefined to deliver mutual benefit? |
| Media switching/addition | Within the current structure, can the Internet reduce costs or add value for some communications? Consider the e-marketing mix. |

**TABLE 5.1**

**Evaluating potential changes to the market map/value chain**

*Participants in the workshop were asked to consider the impact of e-commerce on the life pensions and investment market.*

## 5.3 FINANCIAL SERVICES FUTURE MARKET MAP

Participants in the financial services workshop were asked to consider the impact of e-commerce on the life pensions and investment market and their comments are summarized below and illustrated in Figure 5.3. Similar effects of e-commerce can be expected to occur in other markets.

**Figure 5.3**

**Long-term personal
investment: future market**

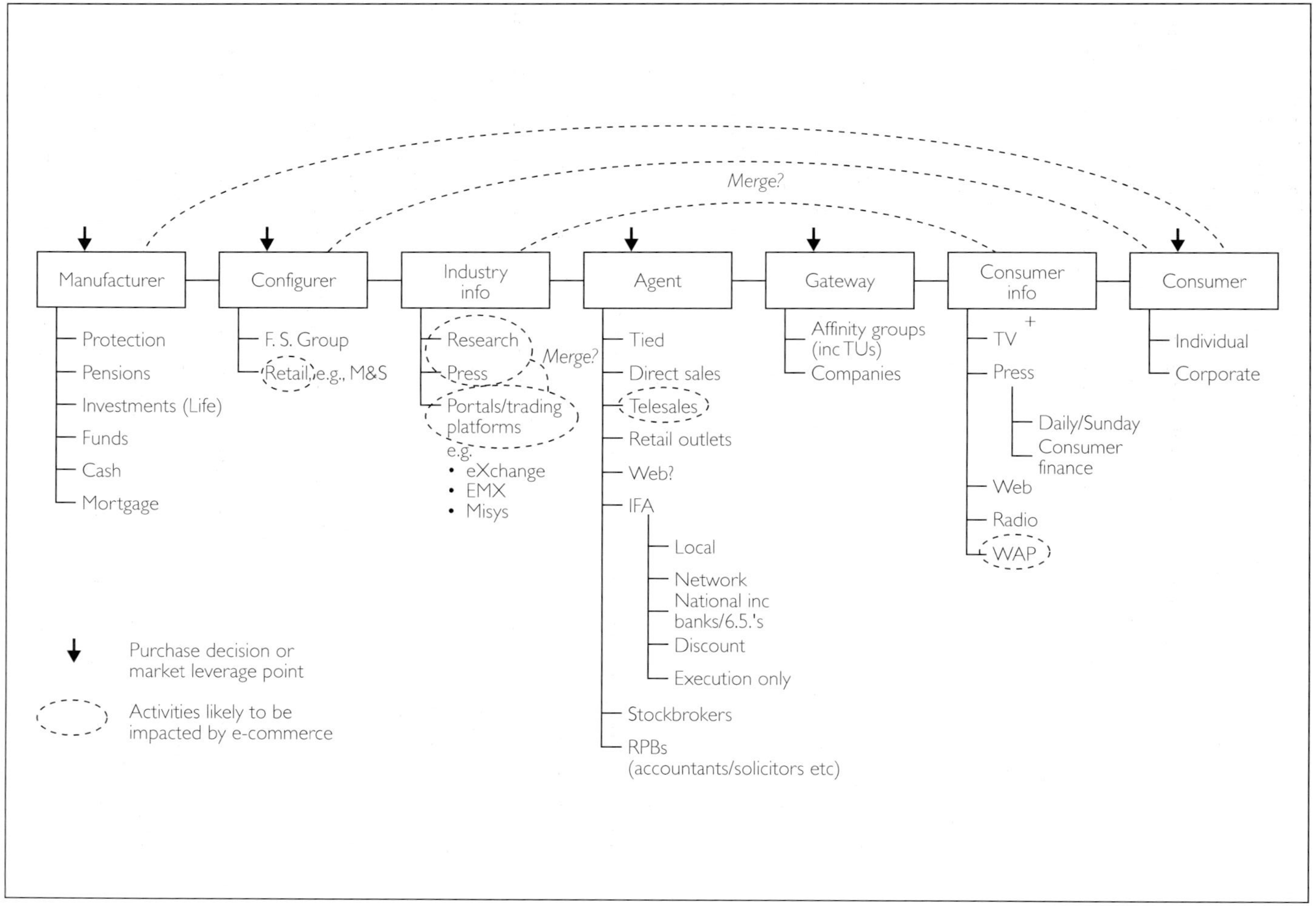

1. *Fund managers go direct.* Fund managers may find that e-commerce makes it easier to sell their products directly to customers. The simplification and transparency of pricing being encouraged throughout the industry should help customers feel more comfortable buying products directly; in fact they may prefer this route since they will not be swayed by an agent who is receiving a large commission for his advice.

   The ability for fund managers to present clear and easy to understand information about their products and their performance online should encourage such direct sales.

2. *The customer becomes the configurer.* Using e-commerce, customers may be able to configure their own investment products from manufacturers. Currently this would be time-consuming and configurers have a significant amount of regulatory knowledge necessary to undertake this function. However, e-commerce applications that contain this regulatory knowledge as 'rules' would allow customers to undertake this function themselves.

3. *There is a blurring of industry and consumer information.* Currently information provided to agents and other professional advisers in the market is quite distinct from that provided to consumers. The former is more detailed and may require specialist knowledge to understand. However, there are already signs of this blurring happening with insurance exchanges, such as eXchange, eMX and Misys, that have traditionally been wholesale or trade exchanges now providing e-commerce routes to end-consumers.

4. *Affinity groups may become trusted portals.* Consumers in the online world are expected to 'join' communities of interest, such as ThirdAge.com, a community for over-sixties. Such communities may be the route that many choose to buy goods and services online.

5. *There will be a 'dumbing down' of advice.* Currently many people wishing to buy investment products turn to a well-trained and regulated financial adviser. With e-commerce, a rise of electronic agents offering advice is likely. These will be rule-based algorithms that base product recommendations on the answers to a few simple questions. However, there is a chance that some such systems will be over simple and will result in customers buying the wrong products.

6. *e-Commerce could result in greater product switching.* The ease of purchasing products via e-commerce, particularly with interactive TV

that provides for follow-through sales, may lead to greater impulse buying and hence greater switching when a customer realizes that they have bought an unsuitable product. This is not only unsatisfactory for customers, who stand to lose financially if they withdraw from products aimed at long-term investment, but also for suppliers since they will face a significant administrative burden.

7. *e-Commerce may cause cycles in consumers' buying patterns.* In the short-term, many online consumers may be tempted to buy direct from manufacturers. However, after time some may find that they made the wrong decision, have accumulated a significant sum and now want to protect it, or are suffering from information overload. These factors may cause them to go back to using advisers in their investment decisions.

   A pattern similar to the one described was seen recently in the US where many consumers transferred to no-load (no upfront fee) funds in which they made a lot of money. They then needed advice on how to ensure these large sums of money were protected.

   Another factor resulting in a cyclic approach to financial advice is that of market conditions. Advice is often seen as less important in a rapidly growing bull market, since anyone can invest and make money. However, as markets begin to slow down, consumers will return to sound sources of advice.

8. *Smaller players are more nimble.* Evidence of this in the investments market is already being seen with smaller IFAs adopting e-commerce services ahead of larger chains.

9. *e-Commerce encourages customers to serve themselves but will not remove face-to-face contact.* By encouraging customers to use online services to register a change of address, or enter bank details, or modify premium amounts, customers are effectively undertaking some of the administrative burden of the agent or manufacturer. However, customers that choose to seek advice will still demand face-to-face contact with advisers, particularly for more complex products.

# 6

# Prioritization and selection

## 6.1 OVERVIEW

The transition to a future vision cannot be accomplished at once, and the organization may not be able to take advantage of all the potential opportunities in the industry. In this stage of the process, options are prioritized and selected (*see* Figure 6.1).

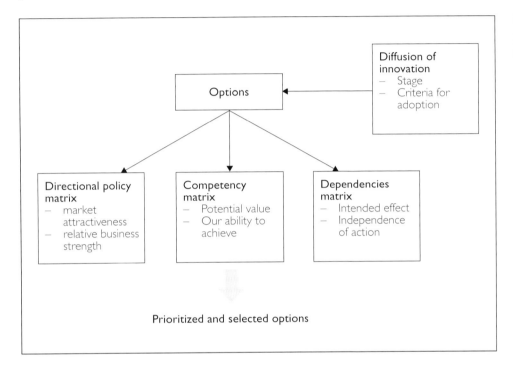

Prioritized and selected options

**FIGURE 6.1**

**Prioritization and selection stage**

*The organization may not be able to take advantage of all the potential opportunities in the industry.*

The options for the organization's adoption of e-commerce generated in the previous stage are evaluated using one or more of a range of tools. The *directional policy matrix* examines the attractiveness of a product-market against the organization's current and potential strength. It can be used in this context to examine the impact on an organization's market position or strength of e-commerce developments in this market and to take investment decisions that account for the product-market's attractiveness. The *competency matrix* compares the potential value of an initiative with the organization's ability to carry out the initiative. The *dependencies matrix* looks at how dependent the organization is on others in order to carry out the initiative. The rate of take-up of e-commerce within an organization's target market, which will have a significant impact on the prioritization of opportunities can be understood in terms of the *diffusion of innovation* curve.

The following sections describe the directional policy matrix, the other suggested matrices and the diffusion of innovation as applied to use of the Internet for e-commerce.

## 6.2 DIRECTIONAL POLICY MATRIX

**Purpose:** To provide a rational basis for resource allocation between different product-markets.

**Description:** Different product-markets within an organization or business unit are compared against three criteria (Kotler, 1994 and McDonald and Wilson, 1999b):

- *Relative business strength*: How good the company is at satisfying customers, compared to the competition. One approach is to use the value curve data discussed above, and to compare the total of the company's scores against the total of the best competitor's. The scores should be weighted against the relative importance of the various criteria to the customer.

- *Market attractiveness*: How attractive the product-market is compared with others. Typical criteria include market size, growth and profitability.

- *Revenue* from the product-market, which is reflected in the circle size.

All other things being equal, a product-market in the *top left* of the matrix should be invested in to grow the market share. The value of a high share in a fast-growing market will be even greater in the future, when the market is larger, than it is now, so it makes sense to invest for the future. In the *bottom left*, the market position should typically be maintained: these product-markets can be a good source of cash to fund the sources of future growth, so should be looked after though not excessively 'milked' or, on the other hand, invested in too heavily. The *bottom right* quadrant should be managed for cash, which may involve cessation or divestment, or just profit-taking. The *top right* quadrant involves selective investment in those product-markets where the company judges that it can move the position leftwards. Figure 6.2 illustrates the directional policy matrix.

**Adapting the tool for e-commerce:** Where most product-markets depicted on the portfolio are entirely new to the company, as may be the case with e-commerce, it may be more valuable to use circle size to represent the current market size rather than our sales. The criteria for the vertical, market attractiveness axis may differ from the conventional trio of market size, growth and profitability: measures of risk, for example, may be important. Certainly, in looking at these criteria, it will be important to look ahead at an estimate of future size, growth and profitability, as the purpose of the axis is to look at the potential for future growth in profits.

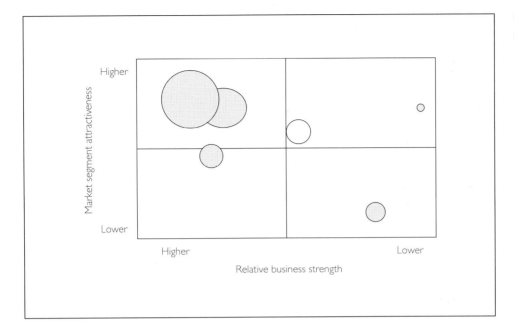

**FIGURE 6.2**
**Directional policy matrix**

## 6.3 COMPETENCY MATRIX

An alternative matrix that can be used to aid organizations in their prioritization and selection of the options generated by the earlier stages of the strategy development process is the competency matrix. This matrix compares the potential value of an initiative with an organization's ability to develop and implement it. This is similar to the directional policy matrix discussed in the previous section, except that it considers the nature of the opportunity in more detail and the organization's ability or competence to develop the service rather than its current business strength.

Figure 6.3 shows the competency matrix and indicates the range of opportunities that an organization may identify using this framework. Obviously the focus of development should be opportunities that are identified as of high value and are relatively easy for the organization to deliver. However, consideration should also be given to opportunities in other quadrants of the matrix. Opportunities that are identified as of lesser value but are easy to deliver may provide a basis for the organization to gain experience with e-commerce. Such opportunities are often low risk and hence can provide a starting point for an organization's e-commerce developments. Such simple opportunities are often termed 'quick wins'.

*The focus of development should be opportunities that are identified as of high value and are relatively easy to deliver.*

Figure 6.4 illustrates a range of potential e-commerce opportunities and shows that such starting points are often simple, static websites or developments internal to the company such as intranets.

**FIGURE 6.3**

**The competency matrix**

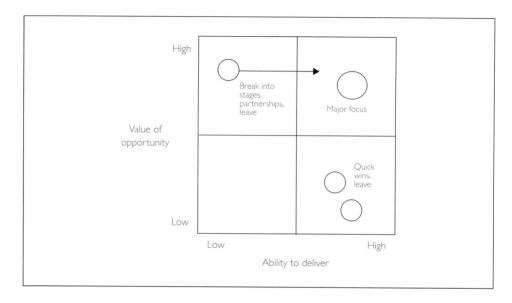

**FIGURE 6.4**

**Potential e-commerce opportunities**

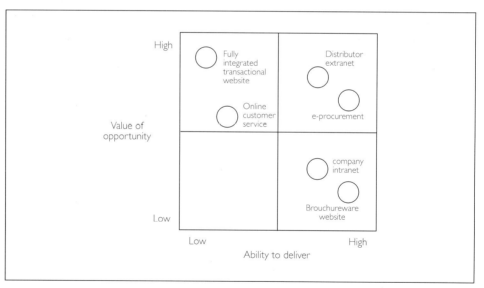

Opportunities that are identified as of significant value to the organization but are difficult to deliver are the most challenging. There will be many reasons why such projects are difficult to deliver. There may be technical challenges to such projects. For example, if organizations want to effectively operate transactional websites, it is necessary to integrate these into their existing order processing and dispatch systems. However, it is likely that many of the challenges are not technology-related or even related to limited resources. Rather, they are likely to be related to the need to change how the organization works and its consequent implications for organizational culture.

Figure 6.3 shows a number of strategies that may be adopted with such projects. The company may be able to break such projects into a number of stages. Some of these may be easier to deliver and although not providing the value of the complete project, allow learning or experience to be gained that enables the company to proceed with further stages of development. An different approach to such opportunities is for companies to partner with organizations that can provide the competencies that they lack themselves. Further exploration of opportunities that may require the involvement of other parties is provided by the dependency matrix.

## 6.4 DEPENDENCY MATRIX

Having identified strategic options, it is also necessary to identify if it is possible to pursue these options alone or if the involvement of third parties is required. These third parties may be technical suppliers, such as software or hardware suppliers, or may be other players in the market map that are influential in the purchase of the products and services under consideration. The dependency matrix is illustrated in Figure 6.5.

| Intended effect(s) | Degree of independence of action | | |
|---|---|---|---|
| | Can do it alone | Need to involve partners | Depend on a third party |
| Win business in target segments | | | |
| Extend customer base | | | |
| Major product/ service enhancement or 'new' product | | | |
| Major cost reduction – transactions – infrastructure | | | |
| Business/brand protection by new e-commerce business but retain old means | | | |
| Avoid significant loss of profitable business | | | |

**FIGURE 6.5**
**Dependency matrix**

*The adoption of any new technology can be considered in terms of Everett Rogers' classic diffusion of innovation curve.*

## 6.5 DIFFUSION OF INNOVATION

The adoption of any new technology can be considered in terms of Everett Rogers' (1962) classic diffusion of innovation curve. McDonald and Wilson (1999a) have used this diffusion curve to map the adoption of the Internet, as shown in Figure 6.6. They separate use of the Internet by consumers in their own homes and its use in the workplace. They also identify four distinct phases of Internet use: experimentation, information gathering, use as an additional channel and use as a main or primary channel – and indicate that these uses are at differing levels of adoption.

**FIGURE 6.6**

**Internet diffusion of innovation**

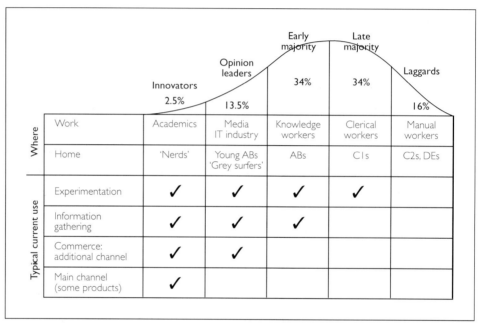

*Source*: McDonald and Wilson (1999a)

The diffusion of innovation analysis can be applied to use of the Internet at a number of levels, such as a country, an industry or a segment. The US, for example, now has over 150 million Internet users, representing around 60 per cent of the population (for statistics on web use see www.nua.org/surveys), placing it past the peak of the curve in basic connectivity, while the UK has around 23 million users, representing the early majority stage. But as Figure 6.6 illustrates, different industries and segments are at different locations on the curve. Symonds (1999) mapped different industries against time, using data from Forrester Research, and finds that early adopters include the IT and defence industries, while Travis (1999) reported, for example, that while a third of ABs in the UK were online, only 2 per cent of DEs were. Merely being connected to the Internet is also of course only the first stage in an increasing reliance on the medium, with only around 10 per cent of the UK population buying actively as yet (illustrated by the ticks in Figure 6.6).

Daniel (1998) explored the characteristics of e-commerce services that affect their rate of adoption, applying criteria from Rogers (1962) and Ostlund (1974) to the example of online banking. The criteria explored are:

1. relative advantage
2. compatibility
3. communicability
4. divisibility
5. complexity
6. customer's perceived risk.

A product which has a relative advantage over existing or competing products, that is compatible with existing norms, values and behaviours, that is communicable, and that is divisible (i.e., can be tried or tested on a limited basis) will diffuse more quickly than others. A product that is complex, i.e., difficult to understand or use, diffuses more slowly than others. A high perceived risk can also slow the diffusion or uptake of a new technology.

Daniel's fieldwork showed that these classic criteria had a good fit to the case of online banking. Consideration of compatibility with previous habits, for example, threw up some of the reasons why people go shopping which were not addressed by the online experience, which include playing a role such as that of the housewife, providing a diversion, taking exercise and meeting people. This analysis had implications for which segments were likely to be late adopters, while also generating debate on ways of providing equivalent experiences online, such as through chat facilities. She also showed how the characteristics of buyers change between opinion formers, who may be prepared to experiment with online banking for the experiment's sake and wrestle with technical difficulties, and the early majority, who require a solid product/service advantage over alternative channels and will not put up with extra costs such as technical failures.

# 7

# Change management

## 7.1 OVERVIEW

Chosen projects now need to be planned and implemented, including necessary changes to the way the organization conducts business as well as IT developments. Two key tools are proposed to manage this implementation process. The *applications portfolio* categorizes IS/IT investments according to their contribution to the business strategy, and enables the appropriate project management approach to be adopted to improve the likelihood of success. The *benefits dependency network* works backwards from the project's objectives to ensure that all necessary business and IT changes are made, to deliver the specific benefits expected from the investment. The change management stage is summarized by Figure 7.1.

*The* applications portfolio *categorizes IS/IT investments according to their contribution to the business strategy.*

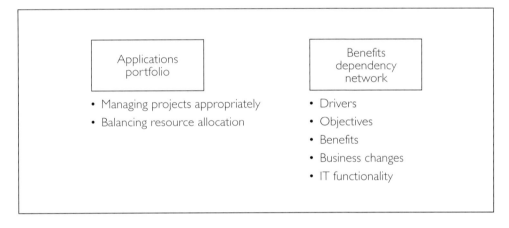

**FIGURE 7.1**
**Change management stage**

## 7.2 APPLICATIONS PORTFOLIO

**Purpose:** The applications portfolio (Ward and Griffiths, 1996) enables management to assess an organization's investments in IS/IT according to the nature of their contribution to the business strategy, and then to resource and manage them accordingly. An adapted version of the portfolio specific to e-commerce was developed during the study and is illustrated in Figure 7.2. Similar approaches to the consideration of e-commerce investments, allowing them to be viewed individually and as a portfolio have been proposed by others such as Hartman and Sifonis (2000).

**Description:** Any of the four segments of the matrix can include e-commerce investments, given the range of business benefits potentially achievable. In a rapidly emerging and evolving aspect of IS/IT development such as e-commerce, the portfolio as above can be adapted to help incorporate the degree of learning involved and also address the risks associated with new technology and business uncertainty. In particular, the development of a new technology and IS/IT service infrastructure is a core enabler of a viable and coherent e-commerce strategy. The key activities involved in both understanding the different contributions e-commerce can make and managing the inter-related contributions are suggested in Figure 7.3. In particular the increased R&D required, experimentation via pilots/prototypes and 'market testing' of concepts, is more specifically addressed. In the field of e-commerce, investment risk is greater since we know less and the nature of the changes involved is less understood.

**Figure 7.2**

**The e-applications portfolio**

| Strategic | High potential |
|---|---|
| e-commerce investments which are *critical* to sustaining future business strategy | e-commerce investments which *may* be important in achieving future success |
| e-commerce investments which are *essential* to remain competitive | e-commerce investments which *deliver improved performance* but are not critical to strategy |
| Key operational | Support |

*Source:* Ward and Griffiths (1996)

In order to both reduce the risks of e-commerce investments and gain benefits available earlier the extended version of the applications portfolio has been developed and is shown in Figure 7.3. This suggests how, starting with technology R&D, a strategy can be defined to both accelerate the organizational rate of learning and reduce any associated risks.

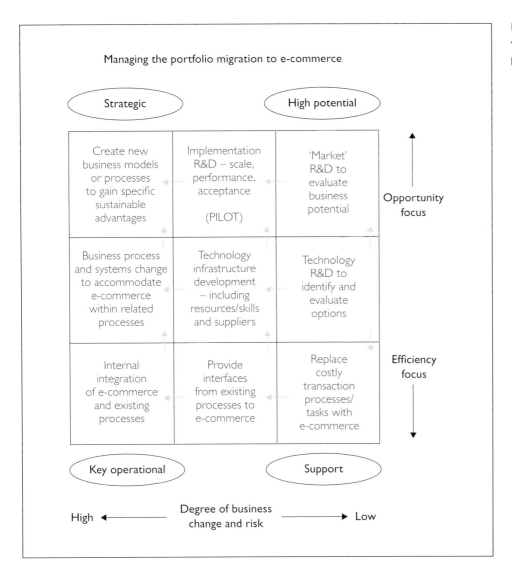

**FIGURE 7.3**

**The extended applications portfolio**

## 7.3 BACON & WOODROW ONLINE!

Bacon & Woodrow is the largest independent partnership of actuaries and consultants in Europe, with 1,100 partners and staff. The firm specializes in helping clients with financial matters that require the modelling of assets, liabilities and risks. The firm's main areas of expertise are: pensions and employee benefits, the financial services sector and the development of investment strategies.

*ONLINE! demonstrates how one system may cover a number of areas on the portfolio.*

ONLINE! is a web-based source of information on pensions. It is aimed at company pension fund trustees and managers and others interested in having access to authoritative information on pensions. The service, which is not restricted to actuarial clients of the firm, currently has over 500 users. The service is also an important tool for staff within the firm.

ONLINE! demonstrates how one system may cover a number of areas on the portfolio. It will prove a useful platform for future business and should therefore be categorized as strategic, but currently the nature of that future use needs further evaluation, and it is therefore high potential. Since the system is used extensively within the firm by the actuaries to do their day-to-day work, it could be considered as key operational. However, if it did not operate for a number of days, paper copies of all documents could be produced and circulated. It could therefore also be classified as a support system (*see* Figure 7.4).

**FIGURE 7.4**

**The applications portfolio applied to Bacon & Woodrow ONLINE!**

| Strategic | High potential |
|---|---|
| Firm wishes to be an e-business and ONLINE! offers a platform for this transaction | Allows communication with customers not previously possible – but need further exploration of the benefits of this new possibility |
| Used by actuaries in their day-to-day working | Offers cost reduction by eliminating paper and time – but if not working could be replaced by paper |
| Key operational | Support |

This diversity of views suggests that the firm should not think of it as a single system but recognize that it has separate parts or elements and that these are likely to need managing in different ways and even by different teams. For instance ONLINE! is clearly capable of supporting cost reduction activities of a support nature (but this would have to be accompanied by Bacon & Woodrow personnel agreeing to work in consistent ways because it is the variety that creates the costs). It is already being used in a key operational manner because some users now need it for their day-to-day business activities. It has high potential because it opens up a degree of communication not hitherto available, but controlled trials of this potential are needed before contemplating rollout. Lastly, given the company's strategic intention to be an active e-business, ONLINE! is an obvious platform for achieving this, but clarity is required from senior executives as what their vision is of an 'e-B&W'.

*A driver is a view by top managers as to what is important for the business.*

## 7.4 BENEFITS DEPENDENCY NETWORK

Benefit dependency analysis seeks to model a programme of IT-enabled change within an organization in such a way that the desired benefits of that change are realized. It is a core technique in the overall process of securing the maximum benefits from all types of IT investment and other types of change programmes (Ward and Murray, 2000). The analysis is presented in the form of a 'benefits dependency network' shown in Figure 7.5.

The main elements of the network are as follows:

- *Drivers* of the project are defined (not shown in Figure 7.5). A driver is a view by top managers as to what is important for the business, such that the business needs to change in response. In the case of e-commerce, such drivers may be either a threat or a new opportunity.

- It is then necessary to establish the *investment objectives* of the specific project or programme. These are agreed statements of what the project under consideration will contribute to an effective response to the business drivers.

- The detailed *benefits* expected from meeting the stated investment objective are then elicited. Additionally, who will receive these benefits and how they will be measured will be identified.

- In order to achieve benefits, it is necessary for people to work in different ways, and it is these changes that are captured in the *business changes* part of the network.

- Other changes may also be required, perhaps before the system can be implemented or used or to enable the identified new ways of working, and these are termed *enabling changes*.

- It is only when this analysis has been carried out that the *IT/IS functionality* required to achieve the business changes, and hence the project's objectives, is defined.

**FIGURE 7.5**

**Benefits dependency network**

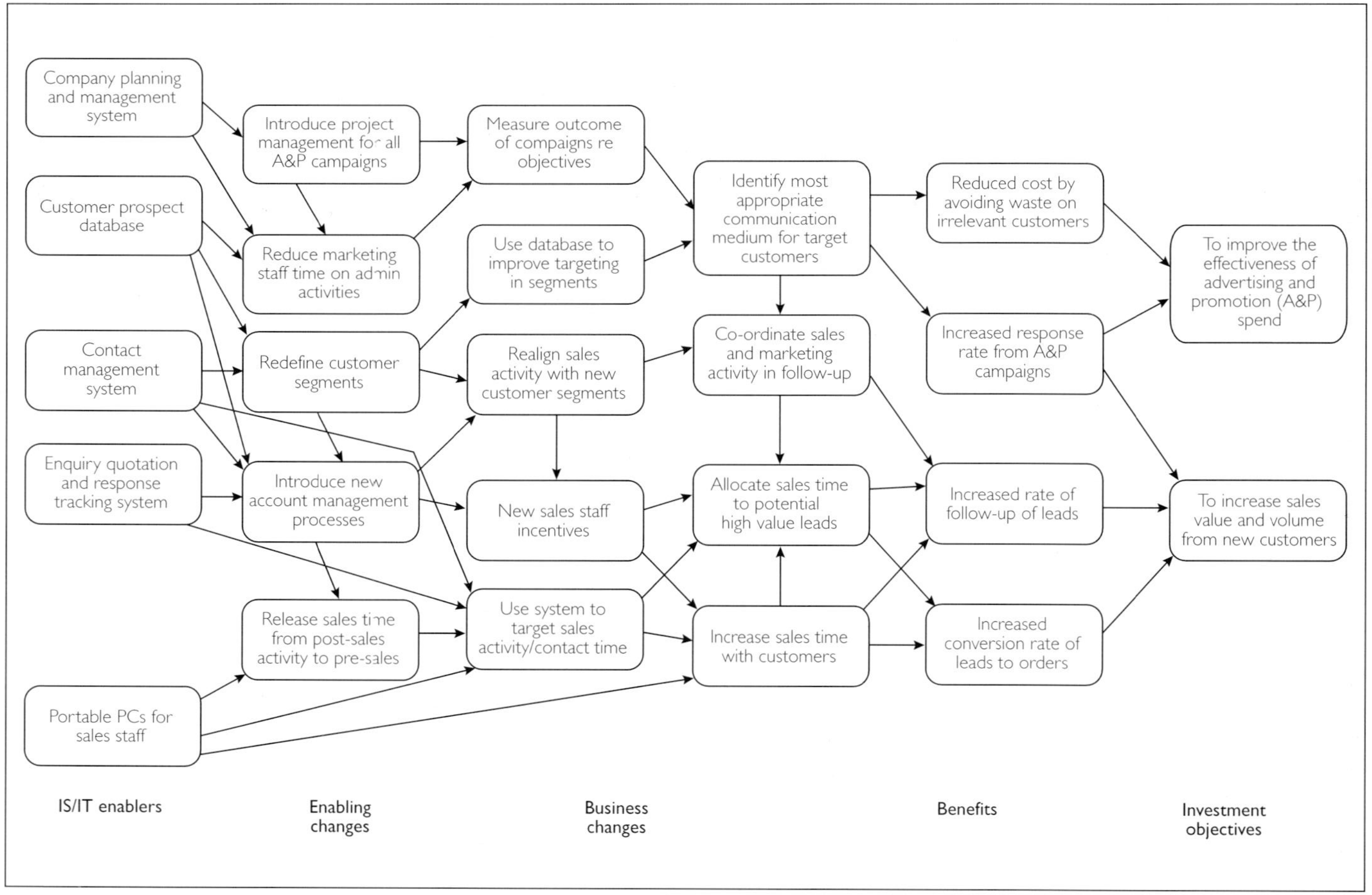


*Source*: Ward and Murray (2000)

- Finally the network is 'connected up' to assess the feasibility of bringing about all of the necessary changes required to deliver the desired benefits. Key dependencies are identified to ensure actions can be taken to avoid losing or delaying the potential benefits.

## 7.5 BUSINESS-TO-BUSINESS OPPORTUNITIES FOR A GREETINGS CARD PUBLISHER

In order to explore the utility of the benefits dependency network (BDN) in the development of e-commerce strategy, a network was developed of a card publisher's project to provide a web-based ordering service to retailers. The network developed is shown in Figure 7.6 and full details are given in the case study (*see* section 10.2).

The objectives of the project were to maintain and enhance the product differentiation and image of the card publisher, to match and surpass the service offered by their competition, especially for small retailers and also to increase the turnover and profit of the company.

A significant number of benefits of such a system were identified and are shown in Figure 7.6. A corresponding number of business and enabling changes that would be required to realize this full benefits set were also identified.

The major points that arose from the BDN exercise were as follows.

- Many of the business changes rely on the managing director. The need for a new sales appointment was clear. We understand that this has since occurred.

- The next step of a pilot was identified on the BDN. A pilot is needed in order to determine the range and scale of likely benefits to the company of a full roll-out, as well as to flesh out how retailers can best be supported online, and how the organization needs to adapt to complement the website itself. It is important that senior management devotes enough time to the relevant business changes and that this does not become a purely IT exercise.

**FIGURE 7.6**

**Benefits dependency
network: a card publisher's
business-to-business website**

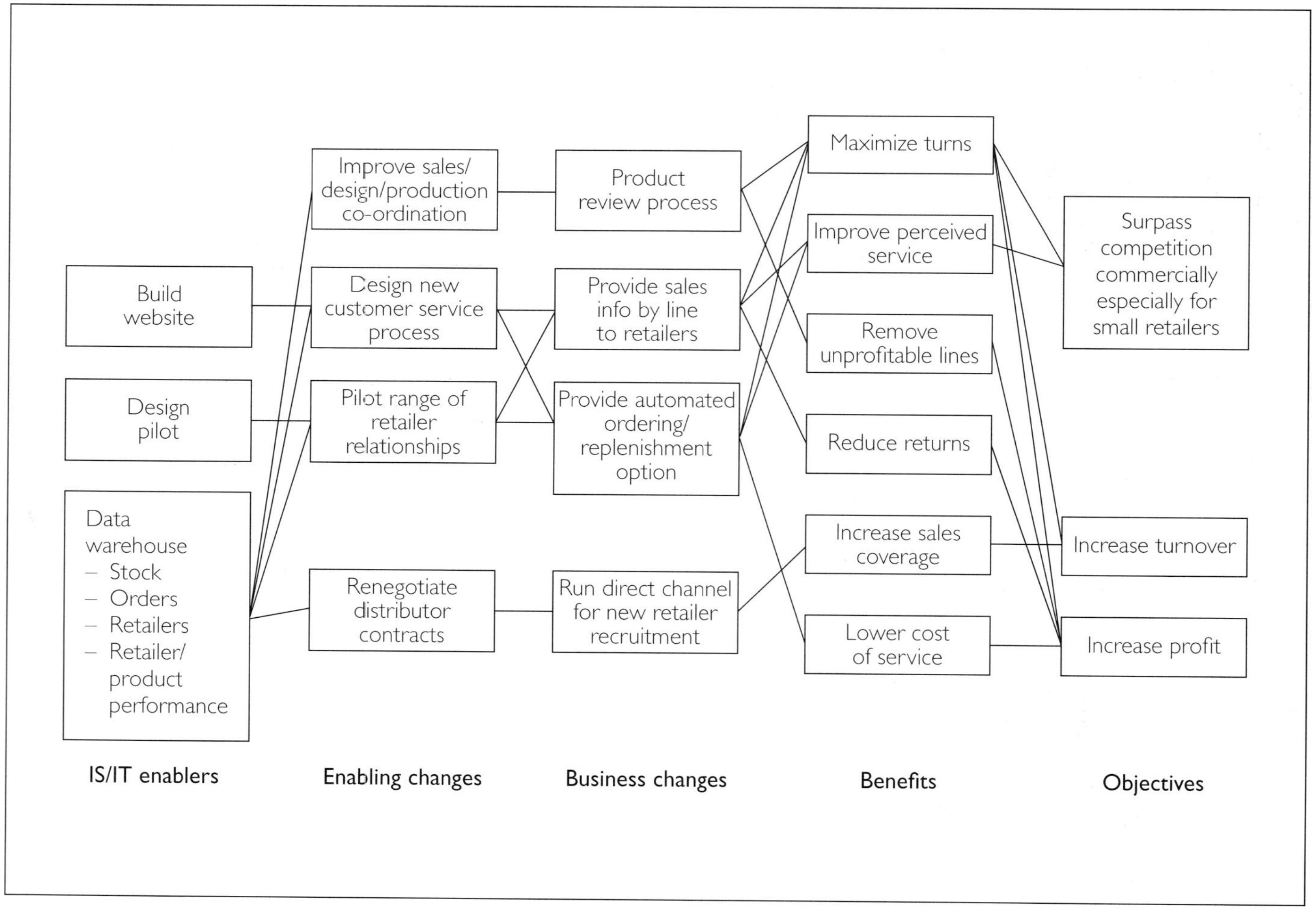

| IS/IT enablers | Enabling changes | Business changes | Benefits | Objectives |

Data warehouse
- Stock
- Orders
- Retailers
- Retailer/product performance

Build website

Design pilot

Improve sales/design/production co-ordination

Design new customer service process

Pilot range of retailer relationships

Renegotiate distributor contracts

Product review process

Provide sales info by line to retailers

Provide automated ordering/replenishment option

Run direct channel for new retailer recruitment

Maximize turns

Improve perceived service

Remove unprofitable lines

Reduce returns

Increase sales coverage

Lower cost of service

Surpass competition commercially especially for small retailers

Increase turnover

Increase profit

The BDN provided a structure to conversations within the firm about what would need to change in the business in order to implement a business-to-retailer web service. This elicited the daunting array of tasks which would need to be performed, and shed light on weaknesses in the management team when these tasks were allocated to individuals. The company should be in a better position to decide whether to proceed with the project in the light of this information, and if it decides to proceed, be better placed to plan the project effectively.

The company had experienced considerable difficulties in the past with new computer systems, due not to the systems themselves as much as the accompanying organizational changes which had not been fully thought-through beforehand. The key strength of the BDN analysis is the identification of the business changes that are required in order to achieve the benefits desired from the IT implementation in question.

# 8

# Measurement of electronic commerce

## 8.1 OVERVIEW

An important part of any strategy development and implementation is the measurement of performance and review of the adopted strategy in light of this performance. Suggested key stages in the measurement of e-commerce projects or services are shown in Figure 8.1. The first stage in this process is to identify the questions that the organization needs to have answered in order to establish if the adopted strategy is indeed the correct one. It is important here not to include questions just because it is known the answers to these already are being measured or can be easily measured. It is equally important not to leave out questions even if the answers are expected to be difficult to obtain.

*It is important not to leave out questions even if the answers are expected to be difficult to obtain.*

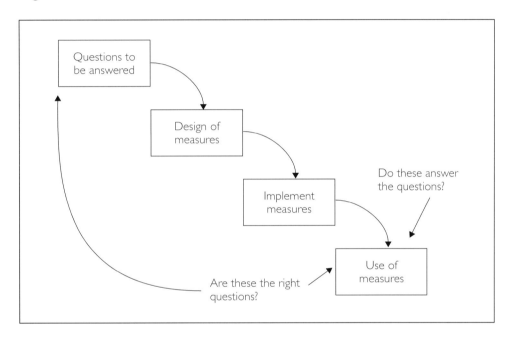

**FIGURE 8.1**
**Measurement stages**

The next stage of the process is to design measures that will provide answers to the questions that have been identified. It is then necessary to implement the measures, that is set up business processes or implement technology solutions that will allow the necessary data to be collected. Following this it is necessary to ensure that full use is made of the information collected. This will involve a stage of asking if the answers to the questions have indeed been provided by the measures developed and implemented and if the right questions were in fact posed at the outset. If necessary it may be necessary to go back and revisit the questions that the organization was trying to answer and devise more appropriate ones.

## 8.2 DEVELOPMENT OF KEY QUESTIONS

In order to guide managers in identifying the key questions that they should pose in developing measures, we suggest that they adopt the performance prism approach.

### The performance prism

The performance prism measurement framework has been developed by the Centre for Business Performance at Cranfield School of Management (formerly at the University of Cambridge) and the Process Excellence Core Capability Group of Andersen Consulting. It is currently being applied to a number of organizations and conditions in order to test its applicability in the field.

The performance prism, shown in Figure 8.2, has five facets that represent five distinct, but logically interlinked, perspectives on performance together with five key questions for measurement design:

**FIGURE 8.2**

**The five facets of the performance prism**

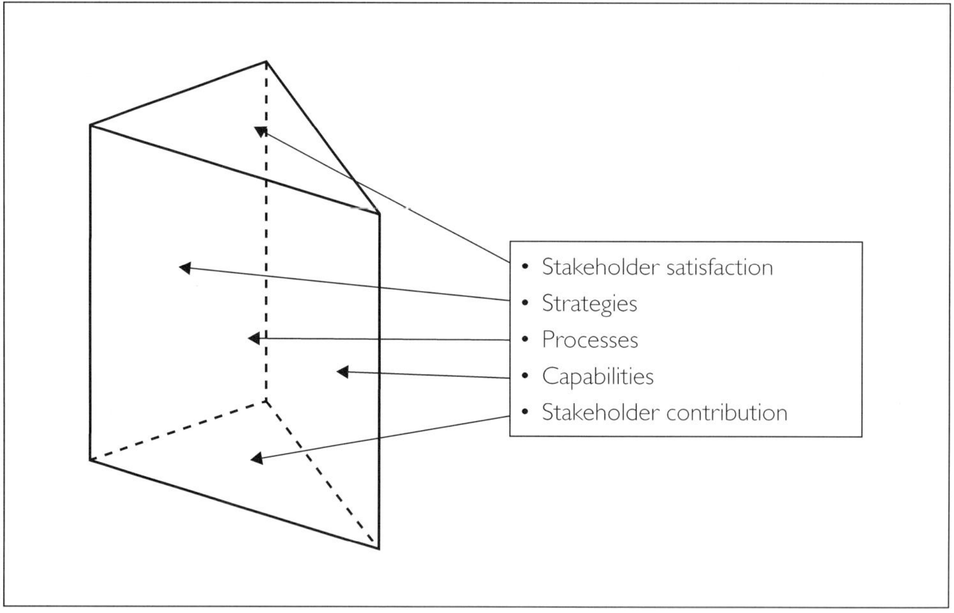

- Stakeholder satisfaction
- Strategies
- Processes
- Capabilities
- Stakeholder contribution

1. *Stakeholder satisfaction*: who are the key stakeholders and what do they want and need?

2. *Strategies*: what strategies do we have to put in place to satisfy the wants and needs of these key stakeholders?

3. *Processes*: what critical processes do we require if we are to execute these strategies?

4. *Capabilities*: what capabilities do we need to operate and enhance these processes?

5. *Stakeholder contribution*: what contributions do we require from our stakeholders if we are to maintain and develop these capabilities?

The first perspective on performance is the stakeholder satisfaction perspective. What managers have to ascertain here is who are the most influential stakeholders and what do they want and need? Once these questions have been addressed, then it is possible to turn to the second perspective on performance – strategies. The key question underlying this perspective is: what strategies should the organization adopt to ensure that the wants and needs of its stakeholders are satisfied? In this context, the role of measurement is fourfold. First, measures are required so that managers can track whether or not the strategies they have chosen are actually being implemented. Second, measures can be used to communicate these strategies within the organization. Third, measures can be applied to encourage and incentivize implementation of strategy. Fourth, once available, the measurement data can be analyzed and used to challenge whether the strategies are working as planned (and, if not, why not).

*Who are the most influential stakeholders and what do they want and need?*

A common reason for failure is that the organization's processes are not aligned with its strategies or, if its processes are aligned, then the capabilities required to operate these processes are not. Hence the next two perspectives on performance are the processes and capabilities perspectives. In turn, these require the following questions to be addressed.

- 'What processes do we need to put in place to allow the strategies to be executed?'

- 'What capabilities do/shall we require to operate these processes – both now and in the future?'

Again, measurement plays a crucial role by allowing managers to track whether or not the right processes and capabilities are in place, to communicate which processes and capabilities matter, and to encourage people within the organization to maintain or proactively nurture these processes and capabilities as appropriate. This may involve gaining an understanding of which particular business processes and capabilities must be competitively distinctive ('winners'), and which merely need to be improved or maintained at industry standard levels ('qualifiers').

The fifth, and final, perspective on performance is a subtle but critical twist on the first, for it is the 'stakeholder contribution', as opposed to 'stakeholder satisfaction', perspective. Take, for example, customers as stakeholders. In the early 1980s, organizations began to measure customer satisfaction by tracking the number of customer complaints they received. When research evidence started to show that only about 10 per cent of dissatisfied customers complained, organizations moved to more sophisticated measures, such as customer satisfaction. In the late 1980s and early 1990s, people began to question whether customer satisfaction was enough. Research data gathered by Xerox showed that customers who were very satisfied were five times more likely to repeat their purchase in the next 18 months than those who were just satisfied were. This, and similar observations, resulted in the development of the concept known as *customer loyalty*. In some organizations measurement and analysis has been taken a stage further and individual customer profitability is computed.

*Gaining a clear understanding of the 'dynamic tension' that exists between stakeholders and the organization is extremely valuable.*

The important point, and the subtle twist, is that customers do not necessarily want to be loyal or profitable. Customers want great products and services at a reasonable cost. They want satisfaction from the organizations they chose to use. It is the organizations themselves that want loyal and profitable customers. So it is with employee satisfaction or supplier performance too. For years, managers have struggled to measure supplier performance. Do they deliver on time? Do they send the right quantity and quality of goods? Do they deliver them to the right place? But these are all dimensions of performance that the organization requires of its supplier. They encapsulate the supplier's contribution to the organization. Supplier satisfaction is a completely different concept. If a manager wanted to assess supplier satisfaction, then (s)he would have to ask: Do we pay on time? Do we provide adequate notice when our requirements change? Do we offer suppliers forward schedule visibility? Do our pricing structures allow our suppliers sufficient cash flows for future investment and, therefore, ongoing productivity improvement? Could we be making better use of the vendor's core capabilities?

The key message here is that all organizations require certain things of their stakeholders and all organizations are responsible for delivering certain things to all of their stakeholders (see Figure 8.3). What drives shareholder satisfaction? *Answer*: dividends, share price growth, predictable results, etc. Unpleasant surprises erode investors' confidence in the management team. What do organizations want of their shareholders? *Answer*: capital, reasonable risk-taking, long-term commitment, etc. This fifth and final perspective on performance – the notion of stakeholder contribution – is a vital one, because it explains why there is so much confusion around the concept of stakeholders in the literature.

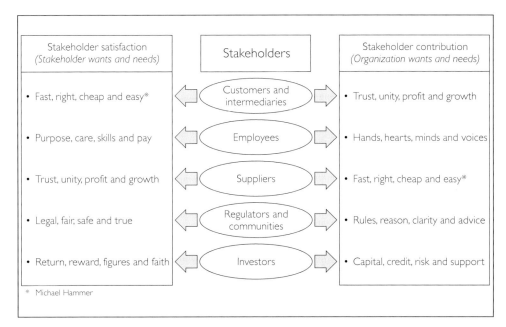

**FIGURE 8.3**
**Stakeholder and organizational wants and needs**

Gaining a clear understanding of the 'dynamic tension' that exists between what stakeholders want and need from the organization, and what the organization wants and needs from its stakeholders, can be an extremely valuable learning exercise for the vast majority of organizations.

## 8.3 DESIGN OF MEASURES

The design of measures can be split into three sub-processes: identification of the data or measures required, an audit of current measures to see if some of the necessary data is already being collected and hence an identification of new measures that must be designed. These three sub-processes are shown in Figure 8.4.

Identification of the data or measures required can be achieved by use of a table as shown in Table 8.1. This sets out clearly the measures needed to answer each of the questions identified. It may be that some measures are used to compute the answers to more than one question.

**FIGURE 8.4**

**Design of measures: sub-processes**

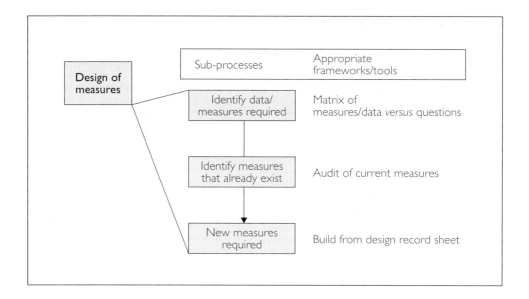

**TABLE 8.1**

**Questions identified and associated measures**

| Questions identified | Data or measures required for each question | | |
|---|---|---|---|
| Question 1 | Measure 1a | Measure 1b | Measure 1c |
| Question 2 | Measure 2a | Measure 2b | |
| Question 3 | Measure 3a | | |

Table 8.1 can then be used to indicate measures that are already being collected in the organization and those which will need to be collected in the future. For measures that are currently not collected, the *Measurement Design Record Sheet* (Neeley, 1999) can be used to design new measures.

## 8.4 IMPLEMENTATION OF MEASURES

*The implementation of measures requires that operational procedures or processes are established to ensure that the required measures are collected.*

The implementation of measures requires that operational procedures or processes are established to ensure that the required measures are collected, at the specified times and frequencies. The measures should then be brought together to compute the answers to the questions identified and the results routinely transmitted to those with responsibility for monitoring the e-commerce venture.

The ease and cost of collecting the required data are important issues to consider when designing the implementation of measures. If either the complexity or cost is too high, it may be necessary to revisit Table 8.1 (Questions identified and associated measures) and consider if there is another way in which the question identified can be addressed.

## 8.5 USE OF MEASURES

As stated above, the implementation of measures should include the development of a process in which the data collected is combined to answer the questions identified and the results are made accessible to those responsible for monitoring the e-commerce development. Ideally the data presented should be in electronic form and capable of being analyzed by the recipient, either in a spreadsheet package or a 'slice and dice' application. Such presentation of the data allows the recipient to explore the data presented to them in their own way. For example if a ratio of interest is outside the range expected or desired, the user of the measures can investigate which parameter is responsible for this and possibly examine the drivers of this in more detail. Electronic presentation of the measures should include records of past data, so that trends can be explored.

Those using the measures should ensure that the data being collected and processed is indeed answering the questions that were identified as being critical to the monitoring and understanding of the e-commerce project. They, or others within the organization should also, from time to time, review the whole measurement set to ensure that the right questions and hence the correct measures are being asked. Too often businesses stick with an existing set of measures because they have become comfortable in measuring these, even though their business may have changed considerably over time.

In this review it is also important to consider if the measurement activity itself is affecting how those in the company are carrying out their activities. Often, particularly when measures are based on a single parameter, activities may have been modified in order to improve the outcome of measure even if it is clear this is not beneficial to the business itself. An example of this is demonstrated in many telephone-based call centres. Companies, keen to maximize the efficiency of their call centres, encourage their staff to take as many calls per day as possible. The result of this is that staff spend as little time talking to customers as possible, in order to maximize the number of calls they can take. By doing this companies are losing out on the opportunity to cross-sell services and products to customers and the ability to gain valuable feedback on their offerings.

## 8.6 SALES CONVERSION ON THE WEB

An example of the design on measures for e-commerce is given by Berthon *et al.* (1996, 1998), who develop a set of measures for use when using the Web as a sales channel, a large part, at least, of the Internet's commercial application. This is summarized in Figure 8.5 and explained below.

**FIGURE 8.5**

**Online sales conversion**

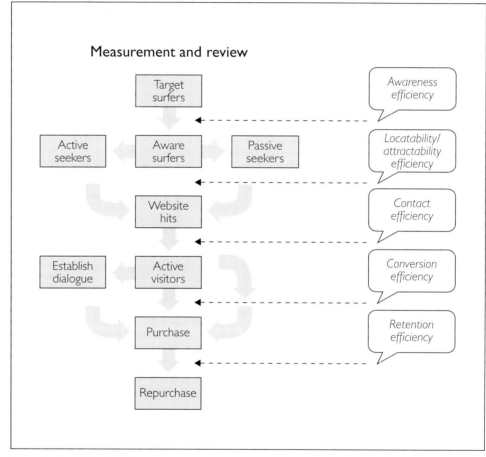

*The first task is to make relevant potential customers aware of the website's existence.*

*Source:* Berthon, P. *et al.* (1996)

### Awareness efficiency

The first task is to make relevant potential customers aware of the website's existence. The first metric represents how well this task is being performed:

$$\text{Awareness efficiency} = \frac{\text{aware surfers}}{\text{target surfers}}$$

'Target surfers' are defined as 'the number of surfers who are potentially interested in the organization's products or services'. This corresponds in traditional terminology to the size of the relevant product-market segment, or perhaps to that proportion of the segment who use the Internet, as other members of the segment must be reached by other means or ignored. 'Aware surfers' are those who are 'aware of its website', without necessarily knowing its exact address. The ratio corresponds reasonably closely to the traditional measurement of awareness as one measure of advertising effectiveness, where awareness is expressed as a percentage of the population (or the relevant segment).

Incidentally, we have reformulated this ratio from Berthon *et al.*'s version. In their 1996 paper the ratio was described as 'aware surfers/surfers', hence ignoring the issue that not all surfers are in the target market for a product-market. The authors attempted to correct this in their 1998 paper to 'target surfers/surfers', which is also obviously incorrect.

## Locatability/attractability efficiency

The next issue is that of making contact with the prospect through him or her 'landing on' the website. The authors distinguish two categories of prospect: those who actively seek to find the website, and those 'passive seekers' whose 'primary purpose in surfing is not necessarily to hit the website'. The meaning of this ratio varies for these two categories. The ratio is:

$$\text{Locatability/attractability efficiency} = \frac{\text{number of hits}}{\text{number of seekers}}$$

For active seekers, this represents the number of those seeking the website who actually find it – the 'locatability' of the website. For passive seekers, this represents the proportion of those prospects which the company has succeeded in attracting to its website while they are browsing – its 'attractability'.

There are various problems with this proposal. One is that the authors have skipped from the concept of 'awareness' to the 'number of seekers' without looking at how the transition from being aware of a website to seeking it might be measured. Another is the difficulty in distinguishing in practice between active and passive seekers. Despite the muddled logic, though, there is promise in the ideas behind it.

## Contact efficiency

The next ratio concerns the distinction between 'hitting' a website, perhaps in passing, and paying an active 'visit' with some serious intent and genuine interest.

$$\text{Contact efficiency} = \frac{\text{number of active visitors}}{\text{number of hits}}$$

The authors suggest two ways of establishing whether a 'visit' has occurred: measuring the time spent on the website, and regarding a stay over, say, two minutes as a visit; and noting whether some interaction between the surfer and the website occurs, such as filling in a form.

## Conversion efficiency

Now we enter more solid ground. While not all websites aim to sell, for those that do, one can measure the percentage of visitors who purchase:

$$\text{Conversion efficiency} = \frac{\text{number of purchases}}{\text{number of active visitors}}$$

## Retention efficiency

We can then measure the capability to turn purchasers into repeat purchasers:

$$\text{Retention efficiency} = \frac{\text{number of repurchases}}{\text{number of purchases}}$$

# 9

# Conclusions

We have proposed a process for the development of e-commerce strategy, incorporating both well-established planning tools and new ideas from the e-commerce field. The areas of this process differing most from traditional planning methods are:

- *The initial, context stage*, which must take account not just of the organization's objectives, but also of relevant aspects of its capabilities.

- *The market vision stage.* Many planning methods skip from an understanding of the industry's current structure to the issue of how the organization should position itself within that structure. The market vision stage adds the important step of predicting how the industry structure itself is likely to be changed as a result of e-commerce, quite independently of what position the planning organization takes towards e-commerce.

    Another new tool suggested in the report is '*value gap analysis*'. This framework examines the value delivered by suppliers and the value required by buyers at each stage of the interactive sales process, in order to illustrate where there is the potential in the buyer–supplier relationship to develop new e-commerce services. This can not only be used to explore the potential for e-commerce between end-consumers and their suppliers, but between any pair of adjacent players in the value chain.

- *The change management stage*, in which the applications portfolio is extended to examine how the portfolio of e-commerce applications should be managed.

In summary, we believe that the Internet neither changes everything nor changes nothing. Our work to date suggests that traditional planning tools such as external value chain analysis, customer needs analysis and portfolio analysis are as useful as ever in generating customer-focused strategies, and checking innovation ideas against market needs. Equally, some subtleties of the online world are difficult to capture using these tools, and hence we have developed new tools, such as value gap analysis or extended existing tools, such as market mapping, in order to capture the unique features of the online world.

The case studies undertaken during this research have allowed us to test the utility of the strategy tools and frameworks. The tools have been shown to be useful, both in the development of new strategies and in the clarification

*The market vision stage adds the important step of predicting how the industry structure is likely to be changed.*

of existing strategies. Examples of the use of the tools are presented in the report, to show their use and aid other companies developing their own strategies in the use of the tool-set.

# 10

# Case studies

# 10.1  SERVING DISTRIBUTORS AT SCHWEPPES SA, SPAIN

## Introduction

Schweppes SA sells its soft drinks to both the grocery and hotel and catering markets. The latter market, termed HORECA, is served by two types of distributor, direct and indirect. Direct distributors receive and despatch orders taken by Schweppes SA salesmen who visit customer premises, such as bars, hotels and discos. Indirect distributors employ their own sales force to deal with customers.

*All distributors, both direct and indirect, are independent of Schweppes SA and distribute exclusively Schweppes SA soft drinks.*

In order to build a closer relationship with their indirect distributors, Schweppes SA have developed an Internet-based system that allows information exchange with them.

An analysis of the dimensions of competence for Schweppes SA has been presented in section 3.5.

## Market mapping

Figure 10.1 shows the market map for the sales of drinks by Schweppes SA in the Spanish market. In the HORECA sector of the market, direct distributors receive orders taken by Schweppes SA's sales people. These sales people visit retail premises (bars, clubs, hotels) and record stocks and requirements by means of hand-held devices. Indirect distributors use their own sales staff and, hence, for this section of the market Schweppes SA has historically had no knowledge of the final customers. All distributors, both direct and indirect, are independent of Schweppes SA and distribute exclusively Schweppes SA soft drinks. They may also distribute other drinks, such as beer or milk, but do not sell competitors' soft drinks.

## The system

The system provides an Internet-based electronic link between Schweppes SA and its indirect distributors in the HORECA market. The system allows distributors to:

- access information about Schweppes SA products

- plan the optimum routing of their sales force

- place orders electronically (the scope of the system will be extended to include electronic payments in the near future)

- access information about promotions

- monitor the level of discounts being offered

- have discounts calculated and paid weekly (previously this was monthly, hence offering cash flow improvement to distributors)

- have the ability to compile reports on their own sales (e.g., by flavour, brand, etc.) by accessing Schweppes SA data warehouse, effectively giving even the smallest distributors access to a sophisticated data warehouse and analysis tools.

**FIGURE 10.1**

**Cadbury Schweppes Spain: current market map**

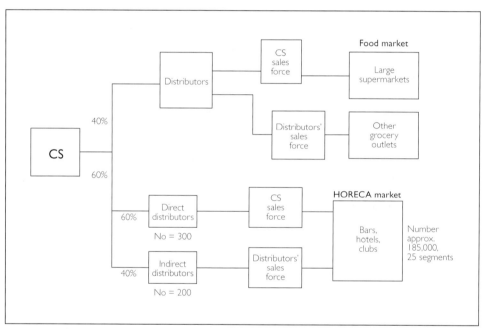

Note: Percentages shown are by volume.

The system provides Schweppes SA with:

- electronic orders from distributors

- information about each customer (e.g., name, address, type of establishment)

- daily sales and stock of each customer (this is supplied weekly to Schweppes SA)

- ability to send promotional and technical information to relevant distributors

- monitoring of discounts offered and taken up.

Perhaps the most significant impact of the system is the provision to Schweppes SA of detailed information about each customer by the distributors. In return, Schweppes SA provides the distributor with a segmentation of their customer base according to Schweppes SA 25 recognized customer types. This knowledge allows both Schweppes SA and the distributors to target promotional activities to the relevant segment, to the benefit of both parties.

The system was piloted with one distributor in June 1999 and is now used by about 20 of around 200 indirect distributors. Some resistance from distributors to share information about their customers with Schweppes SA has been encountered, but the benefits of use have outweighed this concern.

Schweppes SA intend to measure the success of this system by measuring an increased sales volume from their indirect channel, above market growth in this sector (currently around 3 per cent). In future, they believe they may be able to show administrative cost savings from the reduction in paper-based ordering and payment resulting from the system.

## 10.2 BUSINESS-TO-BUSINESS OPPORTUNITIES IN A CARD PUBLISHER

### Introduction

A small, UK-based card retailer wished to explore the benefits and implications of implementing an Internet distribution channel to retailers (both high-street and online), for cards sourced initially from its own stocks but potentially bought in from other card publishers.

### Benefits dependency network for retailer website

A benefits dependency network (BDN) for such a system was developed (*see* Figure 7.6, page 70). A significant number of benefits of such a system and a corresponding number of business and enabling changes that would be required to realize this full benefits set were identified.

The major points that arose from the BDN exercise were as follows.

- Many of the business changes rely on the managing director. The need for a new sales appointment was clear. We understand that this has since occurred.

- The next step of a pilot was identified on the BDN. A pilot is needed in order to determine the range and scale of likely benefits to the company of a full roll-out, as well as to flesh out how retailers can best be supported online, and how the organization needs to adapt to complement the website itself. It is important that senior management devotes enough time to the relevant business changes and that this does not become a purely IT exercise.

*The company had experienced considerable difficulties in the past with new computer systems.*

The BDN provided a structure to conversations within the firm about what would need to change in the business in order to implement a business-to-retailer web service. This elicited the daunting array of tasks which would need to be performed, and shed light on weaknesses in the management team when these tasks were allocated to individuals. The company should be in a better position to decide whether to proceed with the project in the light of this information, and if it decides to proceed, be better placed to plan the project effectively.

The company had experienced considerable difficulties in the past with new computer systems, due not to the systems themselves as much as the accompanying organizational changes which had not been fully thought-through beforehand. The key strength of the BDN analysis is the identification of the business changes that are required in order to achieve the benefits desired from the IT implementation in question.

Once a business-to-business service had been set up, consideration could then be given as to whether there remains a business-to-consumer gap in the UK market, and whether the company is in a position to fill it. At least as importantly, the company could actively support a range of e-tailers who might provide outlets for its cards or images:

1. Gift sites wishing to offer personalized cards to accompany the gift.

2. General shopping sites (e.g., supermarkets) wishing to offer packs of cards to stock up the consumer's stationery drawer or prepare for Christmas.

3. Sites of all sorts wishing to offer e-cards – though competing with well-funded American e-card providers is likely to be hard.

It would seem sensible to start gaining experience by seeking out e-tailers for 1 and 2 above. As well as creating a growth area in its own right, dealing with these customers would help the company if it were to decide to launch its own business-to-consumer service.

The company could differentiate itself from its competitors by helping e-tailers in category 1 by providing an outsourcing service for tailored cards. A printer residing in the e-tailer's fulfilment centre would be used to overprint on to an existing card. Software provided by the publisher could feed the printer with the appropriate text, and also trigger a stock re-order when appropriate. By replicating this model across multiple e-tailers, the company could achieve economies of scale and offer a cheap service to the e-tailer. Even if the gift sites were not given this 'Rolls-Royce' assistance in the first instance, dealing with them would provide valuable learning.

## 10.3  E-COMMERCE STRATEGY DEVELOPMENT FOR YELO LTD

### Introduction

Yelo Ltd, which is based in Carrickfergus in Northern Ireland, designs and manufactures automatic test equipment (ATE). The company has around 30 employees and sells in Europe and the US through local distributors.

The unique selling point of Yelo's test solution is its low cost and flexibility. The company has a high number of highly skilled engineers and, unlike many of its competitors, selling is done by qualified engineers. Customers appreciate that they can have an expert-to-expert conversation with the sales engineers from Yelo.

*The unique selling point of Yelo's test solution is its low cost and flexibility.*

### The automated test equipment (ATE) market

The ATE market is a small part (less than 10 per cent) of the testing and measurement (T&M) market. As with other segments of the T&M market, ATE is dominated by a few multinational organizations (Agilent Technologies, GenRad and Teradyne). Small specialist firms relying on mostly local sales serve the remainder of the market.

ATE customers have a wide variety of production volumes and hence test requirements. Although there is a general trend towards shorter cycle times, some manufacturers specialize in small batches or make frequent changes to their product designs. Such manufacturers require ATE equipment that can be reconfigured quickly and cheaply. Other manufacturers are geared towards the mass manufacture of single products and are more concerned with developing high-speed test solutions to avoid creating bottlenecks in their production lines.

## e-Commerce at Yelo

The objectives of e-commerce adoption by Yelo are: to attract new customers, both in the UK and overseas, to Yelo products and services, to retain existing customers (currently around 70 per cent of business is repeat business) and to help overseas agents to sell Yelo products. In the past it has proved difficult to find agents that are experts at both selling and supporting Yelo products. By providing online sales support to agents, or selling to customers directly online, Yelo could select agents on the basis of their technical support alone.

## Complementary communication channels

It is unlikely at present that many customers will buy specialist technical equipment from a website alone. Customers making such purchases will wish to speak to the supplier because they are often not sure of the exact specifications they require. This dialogue also helps establish the trustworthiness of the supplier in the buyer's mind. A case study on a company called Mansfield Motors (www.mansfield-motors.com), a small business supplying parts and servicing Land Rovers, identified that in addition to using the Web to order parts, these customers also used the phone, fax and e-mail before placing an order. Typically customers contact Mansfield three times regarding each order.

The US high-technology company Lucent (www.lucent.com) has had a similar experience. They have received some online orders worth thousands of dollars with no other contact from the customer, with one order being for $1 million. However, most of their sales enquiries that start online require considerable discussion with the customer, often including a visit from a Lucent engineer, due to the complex nature of the equipment being sold.

Interestingly Yelo's three major competitors, Agilent, Teradyne and Genrad do not currently offer customers the opportunity to buy online. The Agilent site offers a 'buy' button, but when pressed, a list of distributors around the world is shown with their telephone numbers. Currently there is not even an e-mail contact button. Teradyne has a 'get a quote' button, which produces an online form for customers to fill in after which they will be contacted. Similarly, Genrad informs potential customers that their products require customization and asks them to fill in an online form, after which they will be contacted. Yelo should therefore regard their website as one of a number of complementary channels by which they can have a dialogue with customers. As customers become familiar with Yelo and its products, it may be possible for them to order online. A large number of Yelo's sales are repeat purchases and there is more scope for such sales, if they are orders of identical systems to be undertaken online in the future.

## The importance of prepurchase interaction

It should be recognized that in either the physical world or online there are a number of stages in the buying of goods and services by customers. For companies wishing to develop e-commerce services, each stage of the buying process should be addressed. The early stages, when customers realize they have a need, and undertaking and information search (prepurchase interaction) are *more* important for companies to address than providing the functionality to pay for items online (purchase consummation). There are a number of reasons for this:

*Yelo prides itself on the expertise of its engineering staff.*

*   If a manufacturer is not considered by a buyer, or fails to make it on to that buyer's shortlist then no sale will take place.

*   As described above, many customers are not yet ready to buy online and hence spending time developing such functionality is of less use than online services which address the earlier stages of the process.

*   In particular, in business-to-business markets, customers are unlikely to be paying for expensive items by credit card and will use traditional paper-based invoicing.

## Establishing a community

Yelo prides itself on the expertise of its engineering staff and the use of such staff to sell their products differentiates them from their competitors. This approach should be harnessed in Yelo's approach to e-commerce. The website should aim to provide an expert but approachable atmosphere that encourages users to participate. This can be achieved by provision of specialist content (the test guru on the current sites is a good start), threaded discussion groups and bulletin boards. It should be recognized that such activities must be maintained; for example, fresh content must be provided regularly and all e-mail contact must be followed up swiftly. In the Mansfield Motors case, cited above, after about one year their e-mail enquiries were around 200 per week and a dedicated member of staff was recruited to service these.

## Capital equipment is not an issue

Yelo expressed concern that their products are capital equipment and for this reason difficult to sell online. Having studied the evolution of e-commerce and, in particular, examined the sites of other test equipment manufacturers and other similar products, we do not believe that the capital equipment issue will limit online sales in itself. Indeed cars, which would be similarly classified, are currently being sold online (e.g., www.oneswoop.com; www.jamjar.com).

The challenge facing Yelo is that its products are highly technical and that a significant part of them (the fixture and programming) are bespoke. By providing clear information about products online, Yelo will be able to encourage customers to have a dialogue with Yelo, by fax, telephone and even face-to-face if necessary and will be able to ensure this dialogue is of a better quality.

## Online demonstrations

Yelo expressed particular interest in providing online demonstrations of its test systems. Research of websites of similar suppliers has shown that the range of approaches adopted includes webcasts, shockwave and java applications and pdf downloadable data sheets.

## A staged approach – not a quick fix

Any company developing e-commerce services should adopt a staged approach. That is, a simple but robust service should be developed at first. Additional services or features should be added one or two at a time, and user feedback sought and acted upon. Some of the ideas discussed here may be too advanced for Yelo, or its customers, at the present time. It should therefore recognize that these can be stages or steps that will be developed in the future.

The realization that companies should adopt a staged approach to e-commerce, fully understanding the implications of each stage before they move on to further developments, underlines the fact that e-commerce is not a quick fix for businesses. The ease and low cost with which companies can put up a website indicates that undertaking e-commerce can be quick and cheap. However, companies that are building value from their e-commerce services are finding that it takes time and ongoing investment of other resources. In particular, the most successful strategy for traditional companies is one of 'clicks and bricks', that is, one that builds on the existing physical presence, such as properties or salesmen and provides multiple, complementary channels through which to hold a dialogue with customers.

*Yelo should view their e-commerce services as an opportunity to initiate or continue a dialogue with their customers.*

## Summary

Management at Yelo Ltd are concerned that customers are not yet prepared to buy capital equipment online. It is likely that there is resistance to buying such equipment in this way, since it tends to be expensive and there is evidence that buyers, seeing the greater risks involved, and the difficulties of paying online, are less likely to buy expensive items online.

Whilst there is a reluctance to buy expensive items online, it would appear that Yelo's greatest challenge is not the cost of its products but the fact they are bespoke and require liaison between the customer and Yelo's engineers. Yelo should therefore develop online services that aid and improve this dialogue between their engineers and customers, rather than aiming to replace it. They should not consider the number of systems sold online as a measure of success for their e-commerce developments, rather view their e-commerce services as an opportunity to initiate or continue a dialogue with their customers. They should also recognize that this dialogue with customers may utilize a number of different channels. Once again they should not view the e-commerce activities as failing or performing badly, but as in the case of Mansfield Motors cited above, accept that the technical nature of their products will require customers to make direct contact with Yelo's engineers.

A driver for Yelo's development of online sales capability is a wish to increase overseas sales without the need to recruit new distributors. For the reasons given above, it is unlikely that customers overseas will be willing to buy bespoke equipment online, without the advice of a local agent. Yelo should therefore consider developing online tools that will help their overseas agents to sell and maintain their systems rather than aiming to sell without the use of agents.

As customers become more familiar with buying complex and expensive items online, it may be possible for Yelo to sell systems online. In the first instance these are likely to be bought by customers requiring replacement or additional systems who are therefore able to specify exactly what they need. The approach that we have suggested here, that is the development of services to help the dialogue between engineers and customers and to support overseas agents, should be viewed as a staged approach towards being able to sell bespoke engineering systems online.

## 10.4 BACON & WOODROW ONLINE!

### Introduction

Bacon & Woodrow is the largest independent partnership of actuaries and consultants in Europe, with 1,100 partners and staff. The firm specializes in helping clients with financial matters that require the modelling of assets, liabilities and risks. The firm's main areas of expertise are: pensions and employee benefits, the financial services sector and the development of investment strategies.

### Introduction to ONLINE!

ONLINE! is a web-based source of information on pensions. It is aimed at company pension fund trustees and managers and others interested in having access to authoritative information on pensions. The service, which is not restricted to actuarial clients of the firm, currently has over 500 users. The service is also an important tool for staff within the firm.

The information available on ONLINE! ranges from daily updates to records of past legislation, which may have an impact on current schemes. It can therefore be used either to keep up-to-date with industry developments or as a source of reference information.

The service also offers a service called the Web Bookshelf that allows Bacon & Woodrow to work electronically with its clients. This service is restricted to actuarial clients of the firm. It consists of a virtual work area, tailored to each client, where working documents and information relating to the specific scheme(s) of the client can be kept and accessed by appropriate client and Bacon & Woodrow staff. This information can also easily be made available to relevant third parties such as lawyers and auditors.

*The firm recognized that relationships need to be built and maintained at the highest level of client firms.*

## Dimensions of competence

Those at Bacon and Woodrow interviewed as part of this research felt that their employee benefits group had an excellent level of customer intimacy. The firm recognized that relationships need to be built and maintained at the highest level of client firms, and this is being carried out. Individual actuaries also tended to build good relationships with their clients.

The interviewees felt slightly less positive on both the product leadership and operational excellence categories. They felt that actuarial services were seen as fairly similar and therefore it was difficult to differentiate the firm to potential new clients. It was felt that the ONLINE! service would offer an opportunity for the firm to do this, and also offer a platform for it to offer new services to clients.

With regard to operations, it was felt that within the firm, concern about risk led to a tendency to always try and do a perfect job for clients, which made it difficult to predict how long work would take. There was also a feeling that there were many separate voices and activities within the firm, making it difficult for staff to know what is important, in particular in the provision of IT systems. New systems seem to be developed fairly regularly and issued to staff who are not sure how or why they should be using them. The IT group do provide training on all new systems, but actuaries are concerned about using time that could be spent with clients for such training sessions.

Figure 10.2 illustrates the dimensions of competence.

## Business drivers and objectives

One of the major issues facing Bacon & Woodrow is a change in the market as many companies change their pension schemes from defined benefit or final salary schemes to defined contribution or money purchase schemes. This is likely to result in lower volumes of statutory work required, making the firm interested in increasing the amount of consultancy work it carries out in the field of employee benefits. Currently the firm's revenues from employee benefit work is split, with roughly 33 per cent from statutory work and the remaining 67 per cent from consultancy work. In the insurance group within the firm, this split is roughly the other way around, with 40 per cent of revenues coming from consultancy and 60 per cent from other work.

**FIGURE 10.2**

**Dimensions of competence for Bacon & Woodrow**

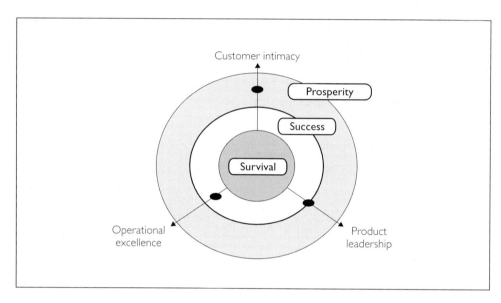

*Bacon and Woodrow currently have a group of staff addressing the total remuneration packages market.*

Nonetheless, despite the interest in growing the revenues from consultancy services in the field of employee benefits, it is recognized that many clients may also require statutory work to be undertaken. It is therefore important for Bacon & Woodrow to be efficient in this latter type of work.

One area of market growth in the future may be in total remuneration packages: advice on how to construct remuneration packages that are optimal for staff and business. Such schemes are usually a mix of salary, share options and other benefits such as health insurance. Bacon and Woodrow currently have a group of staff addressing this market, but there is some belief that this area may grow considerably in the future.

## Benefits dependency network

The benefits are those that might be expected from realizing these objectives. For example, achieving lower and more predictable costs for statutory work, as part of reducing reliance on this work, could result in more projects being completed on time and to budget. Meeting the objective of lower costs could also provide the benefit of costs remaining competitive with other firms, even if the reduction in statutory work in the market means that all firms are chasing less work and fees are reduced.

Meeting the objective of increased consultancy work could result from Bacon & Woodrow winning more new business pitches and developing new products and service offerings in this field. Similarly, developing new products or services, such as electronic commerce-based services that can lock the client into the firm, could lead or encourage clients to work in new ways, attract new clients and also be used to secure existing client relationships.

*ONLINE! clearly has a major role in enabling a number of Bacon & Woodrow's key objectives.*

Figure 10.3 shows the business changes it is expected will be needed to realize the benefits listed. As is often encountered with benefits networks, a number of changes in the way the business currently works are needed to realize the full set of benefits listed. Those identified include: improved use of marketing material, reduced time spent undertaking routine work, increased knowledge of other services the firm offers, the development of new products and services and the creation of a non-actuarial route for cross-selling.

A number of changes, termed *enabling changes*, are necessary to allow the business changes identified to be achieved. These include standardizing processes, in order to reduce routine work, training individuals in knowledge of other services of the firm and even selling training for the actuarial staff, in order to improve cross-selling and the selling of new products and services. The management of information or knowledge is a very common issue, and a number of the business changes identified by the participants require that rigorous information management procedures are adopted throughout the organization. Such procedures include: integrating information collected from different sources, keeping it up to date, removing old material and archiving all material. Such practices are likely to require management by senior staff members and it may be necessary to release them from fee-paying work for this.

## Summary

ONLINE! clearly has a major role in enabling a number of Bacon & Woodrow's key objectives. In particular the following issues were identified:

**FIGURE 10.3**

**Benefits dependency network for Bacon & Woodrow**

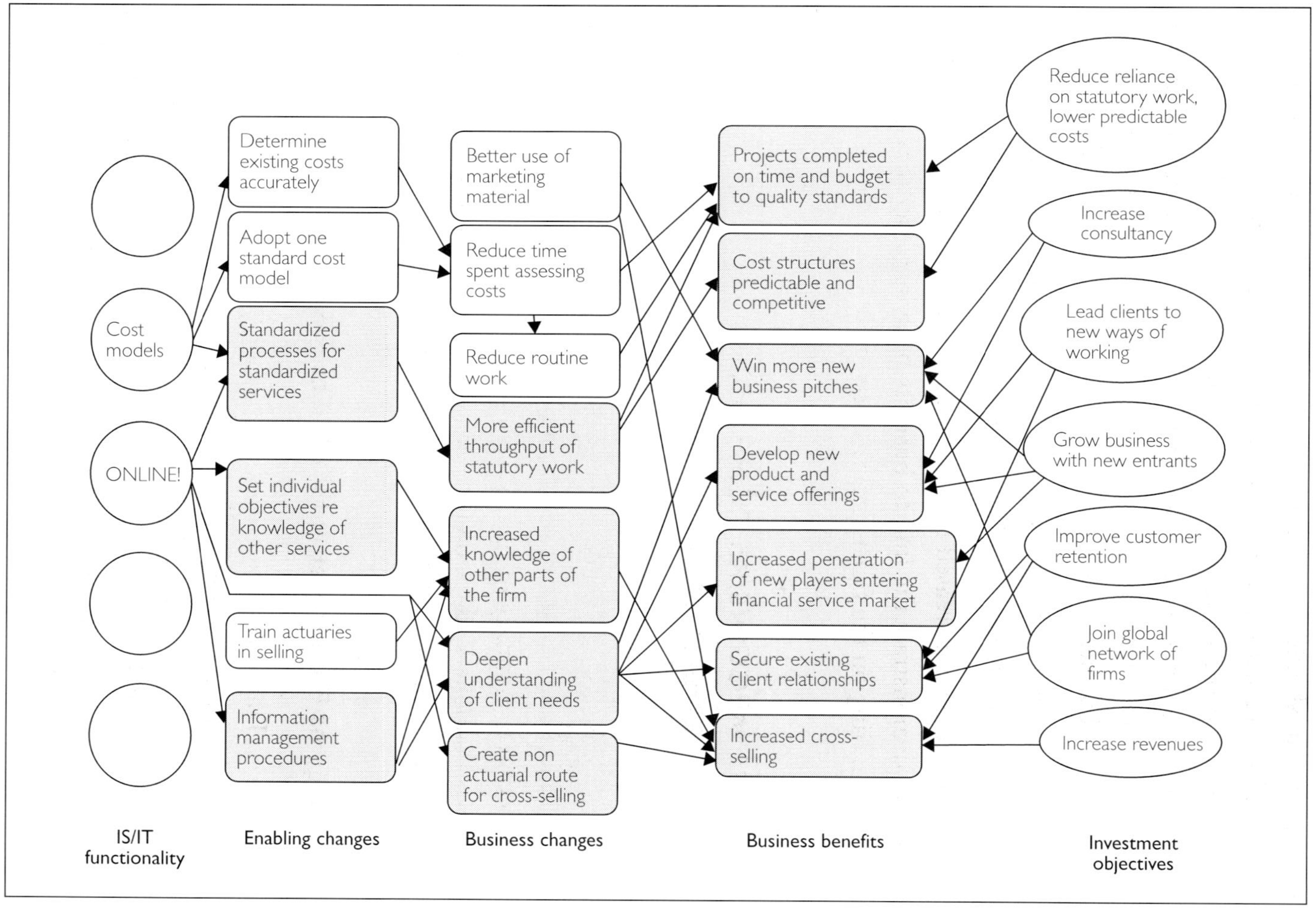

- The system should not be thought of as one single system but it should be recognized as having a number of separate parts or elements. Furthermore it should stop being seen as an 'IT system': ONLINE! is a new way of working for B&W that could support the organization's strategic aims, its ownership should be emphatically within the business and its development controlled from there.

- In accordance with the applications portfolio, it may be necessary to manage those elements in different ways.

- In order to gain increased uptake by clients and consultants, B&W should demonstrate the link to business benefits rather than just concentrating on the functionality of the system.

## 10.5 ARJO WIGGINS/RS COMPONENTS E-PROCUREMENT TRIAL

### Introduction

This study is a summary of Arjo Wiggins' trial of e-procurement with one of its main suppliers, RS Components. The project formed part of their larger implementation of SAP Finance and Procurement software.

### Arjo Wiggins Fine Papers and RS Components

Arjo Wiggins Fine Papers, recently re-organized as Fine & Drawing Papers, is a division of Arjo Wiggins Appleton plc, one of the largest paper manufacturing and merchanting companies in the world. Fine Papers are manufacturers of high quality writing and office papers, together with prestigious paper and board products supplied for the advertising, promotional and PR business.

RS Components (parent company Electrocomponents plc) is the leading high service business-to-business distributor of electronic, electrical and mechanical components serving 1.5 million customers in 160 countries around the world. In addition to the RS Catalogue and their award-winning CD-ROM, they launched the RS website in 1998, giving their customers both an instant choice of over 110,000 products and access to over 15,000 technical data sheets.

## Current purchasing process

The procurement process operated at both company and local level, with the main raw materials such as pulp negotiated and procured internationally, whilst most other items were negotiated and purchased at site level. At the same time as this project, a separate study had introduced companywide buyers, responsible for negotiating and agreeing contracts across all sites.

At local level the role of purchasing had not changed over many years, with the purchasing department concentrating mainly on higher value raw material buying, with individual functions having much autonomy for their own purchasing, such as engineering services and parts, IT equipment and Health & Safety equipment.

## Introduction to the e-procurement trial

Following discussions with RS Components, it was agreed to complete a trial whereby selected members of the engineering department would order non-stock items through the Internet, instead of through the recently installed SAP Purchasing System.

The main objectives of this trial were:

• to identify if Internet ordering could simplify and reduce the time spent on the purchasing process, whilst retaining adequate purchasing controls

• to eliminate the need for uncontrolled telephone ordering without reducing the required speed of response.

Key factors in the decision to trial Internet ordering specifically with RS Components were:

• availability of an Internet ordering system

• proven reliability and usability of the website, enabling users to adapt to the change with confidence

• total acceptance of the proven accuracy and consistency of RS Components' delivery service and corresponding documentation, from both the engineering and finance departments

• A 'no quibble' guarantee, ensuring that any savings made, in reduced processing, would not be erased by subsequent processing of queries.

Without this level of confidence in the supplier's service and support, the trial would not have been practical.

## Basis of the trial

Seven senior engineers were selected to use the system; each of them was then issued with their own access and order value limit. The standard RS website (www.rswww.com) (*see* Figure 10.4), was used without any modification, as it already incorporated all the key data fields required for subsequent invoice processing within SAP. Items to be purchased, valued above the defined limit, were processed through the normal SAP system.

*The standard RS website was used without any modification, as it already incorporated all the key data fields required.*

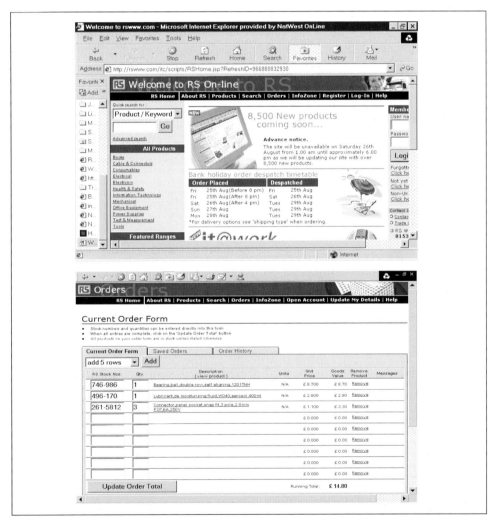

**FIGURE 10.4**
**RS Components home and order page**

For those items purchased through the website, no subsequent entry was entered into SAP until the end of each month, when a summarized invoice was received via e-mail from RS Components. Details from the e-mail were entered manually into the SAP invoice processing system.

The other change to existing practice was that regarding approval and reconciliation. The selected engineers were empowered with more authority, with the tasks of order approval and order item receipting/invoice matching, using SAP, being eliminated. The onus was placed upon trust. Unless an engineer queried the item with the finance department, the invoice would be automatically processed on the basis of full and acceptable receipt.

This represented a major change in working practice, as a single method of purchasing using SAP, with strict controls and procedures in place, had just been implemented. The concept of reducing these controls and operating more on a basis of empowerment and trust between internal departments and the external supplier was somewhat alien.

*Actual processing time was reduced from an average of 40 minutes per order to five minutes.*

The other significant implication of eliminating the SAP order entry was the loss of historical data available within the one system. It was agreed, however, that the reduction of tasks, and other related benefits outweighed the non-availability of purchasing data within SAP.

**Results of the trial**

Figure 10.5 shows the impact on the purchasing process through the introduction of the Internet ordering system. The key savings identified were as follows.

- Waiting time (as shown in brackets) was eliminated. This elapsed time, of up to three days in total, consisted of time awaiting management approval of orders plus the postal delay waiting for the hard copy order to reach the supplier. The delivery lead-time of 24 hours from the supplier was unaffected.

- Actual processing time was reduced from an average of 40 minutes per order to five minutes. Where queries used to arise, especially due to the large percentage of telephone orders, the average processing was actually closer to an hour per order.

- The time spent by senior management, in approving these low-value orders, was eliminated.

- The time required by the finance department to enter invoices manually into the SAP system was reduced from approximately four hours each month to five minutes. Previously, an invoice was received and processed against each order.

**FIGURE 10.5**

**Comparison of processes**

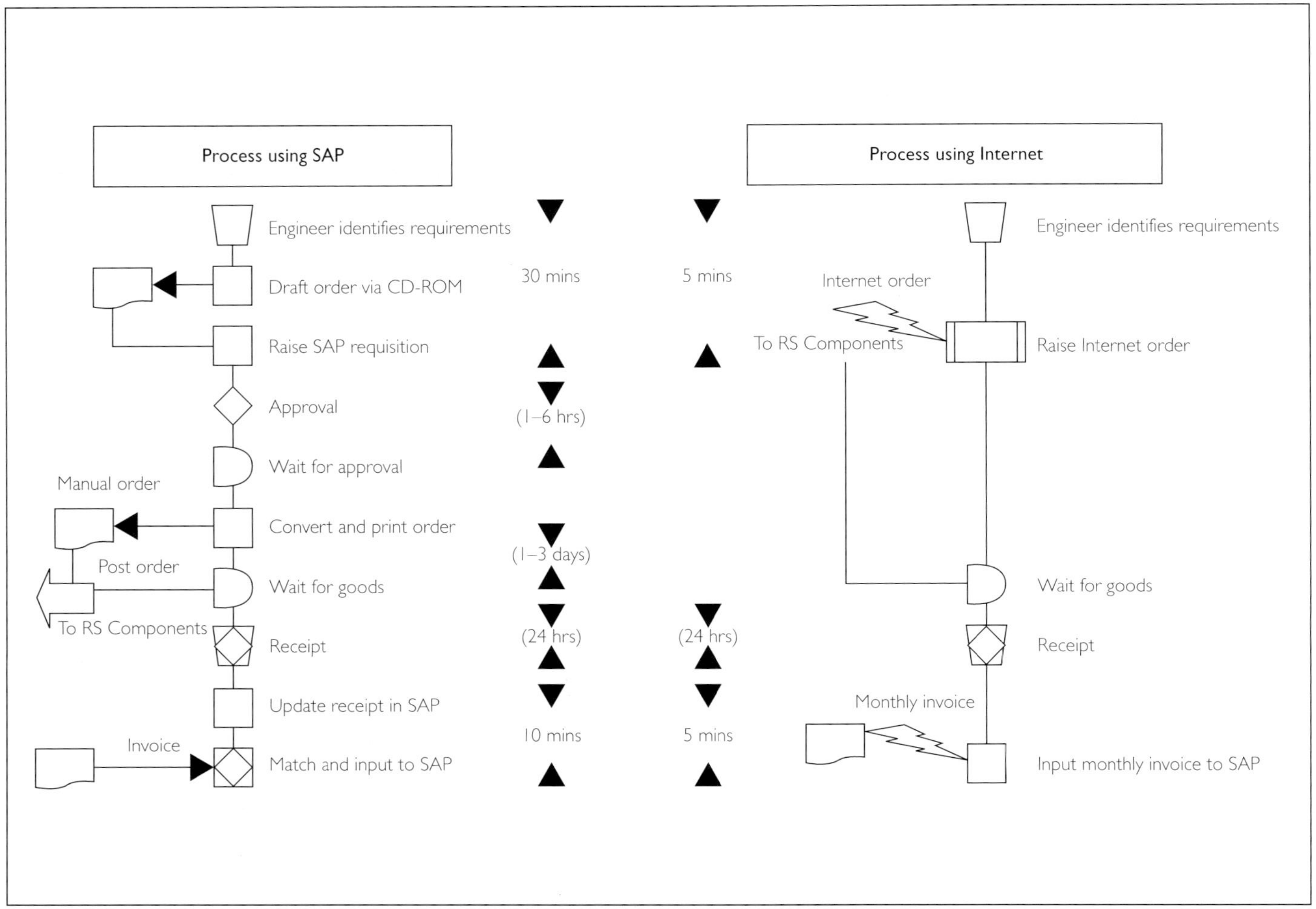

| Process using SAP | | Process using Internet |
|---|---|---|
| Engineer identifies requirements | | Engineer identifies requirements |
| Draft order via CD-ROM | 30 mins | |
| Raise SAP requisition | | Raise Internet order — 5 mins |
| Approval | | Internet order |
| Wait for approval | (1–6 hrs) | To RS Components |
| Convert and print order | | |
| Manual order | (1–3 days) | Wait for goods — (24 hrs) |
| Wait for goods | | Receipt |
| Post order | (24 hrs) | Monthly invoice |
| To RS Components | | Input monthly invoice to SAP — 5 mins |
| Receipt | | |
| Update receipt in SAP | 10 mins | |
| Match and input to SAP | | |
| Invoice | | |

In addition some other, unexpected, benefits were realized during the trial, and these were:

- Expensive downtime on a machine was avoided when a halogen-lamp part was unavailable from local supplier. The part was ordered and delivered from RS within 24 hours.

- Time obtaining quotes for low-cost items from multi-suppliers was eliminated, as the order was placed directly on RS through the Internet. (Savings that could have been made on the parts, from other suppliers, were negated by time needed to complete the task.)

- Ability to review technical information on the online data sheets has helped the engineers solve some problems and helped them to identify, more easily, their actual requirements.

- Errors were almost eliminated, as the graphical images helped the engineer identify the correct items to purchase.

- Because orders were placed only for items, which were shown to be available on the website, part orders were eliminated along with the corresponding queries attached to them.

Although the trial was on a relatively small scale, it has proved successful and achieved its main objective. With some minor improvements to the process and small changes to local responsibilities, the trial could now been turned into working practice and extended, for this particular supplier, to more users, possibly for all low-value items, i.e., for stock as well as non-stock, and to other sites.

## Conclusions

Although the trial has identified that substantial benefits could be achieved through web purchasing, it does not yet offer a total solution for Arjo Wiggins Fine Papers. The wide variety of items purchased and the range of suppliers used mean that a single approach would not be practical at this stage for the following reasons.

- The limited number of suppliers yet to offer web ordering, especially small specialist suppliers.

- Variability and inconsistency of service from many suppliers would limit options for reducing controls, thereby limiting opportunities for achieving savings in processing time.

- The advantages gained through moving to a single procurement system, with its single source of purchasing information would be lost, if use was made of each supplier's own web ordering system. This would be especially relevant to the buying department, who would lose the availability of information on ordering, deliveries, receipting, complaints, etc., and thereby limit their ability to monitor supplier performance.

- Where the items ordered are integral to the production process and determined by the manufacturing requirements planning (MRP) functionality, the opportunity exists to apply different supply methodologies, e.g., consignment stock, just-in-time (JIT), planned delivery scheduling, etc. None of these methodologies could be applied if orders had to be entered through the supplier's website.

*Reducing costs through lower buying prices is of prime importance to all organizations.*

Reducing costs through lower buying prices is of prime importance to all organizations. The Internet offers great opportunities to achieve this. Best price is not the only criterion however, in selecting trading partners. Ability to supply, consistency of quality, acceptability and guarantee of service and administrative process are all fundamental factors in determining the source of supply. These factors cannot be identified through a website. Lower buying prices would soon be negated if late delivery or poor quality affected production.

All of these issues must be taken into account, when identifying the most suitable trading method(s) and partners. There are a variety of opportunities available to help Arjo Wiggins Fine Papers achieve a more effective procurement process. These include:

- online trading between buyer's and supplier's enterprise resource planning (ERP) systems, whether directly or via third party such as Commerce One or SAP

- using seller's Internet site such as RS Components for high-volume, low-value non-specialist items

- eliminating multiple ordering by providing supplier with forward demand/MRP output/forward delivery plan, etc., and moving towards more JIT trading (ideally transmitting this information, via electronic means, would provide the most benefits to both trading partners)

- Agreeing contracts for vendor-managed stock, whether by electronic or manual processes

- Increase use of barcode receipting
- Electronic invoicing, whether by Internet or electronic data interchange (EDI).

## 10.6  IDENTIFYING ROUTES TO MARKET AT SMITHKLINE BEECHAM

*Before a market map can be developed, the market under study needs to be clearly defined.*

### Introduction

SmithKline Beecham (SB) were interested in identifying routes to market in their consumer healthcare business that would contribute to the development of an effective e-business strategy. Focusing on the drinks market, the first part of this case study describes the current market and SB's positioning within it. The later stages of the case consider how the market is likely to change as a result of the adoption of e-commerce technologies.

### Market definition

Before a market map can be developed, the market under study needs to be clearly defined. Market definition is difficult in this particular market because previously relatively distinct drinks markets have been tending to converge, so that quite different products can satisfy a wide range of interrelated needs. Drinking is, for example, a way of satiating thirst, a social activity, a source of nutrition and a means of improving athletic performance. Whilst some products fall into only a single category, it is increasingly common to find products being used to satisfy several of these needs. Consequently, attempts at a needs-based definition found it difficult to avoid excluding consumers with relevant needs, or including those without relevant needs. A broad definition of 'the soft cold drinks market' was therefore adopted. It was noted that SB differentiated its products in this area by demonstrating their value to customers using scientific evidence. It was concluded, however, that this represented a positioning within the wider market, rather than a basis for a market definition.

Whilst hot drinks may, on occasion, be substituted by cold drinks to satisfy a customer's need for a drink at a particular moment, it was decided, on balance, to leave these two markets as distinct.

## Current drinks market

A simplified version of the current market map for the drinks industry is shown in Figure 10.6. SB is one of a number of drinks manufacturers, selling both directly to retailers and via distributors – wholesalers and cash and carry stores.

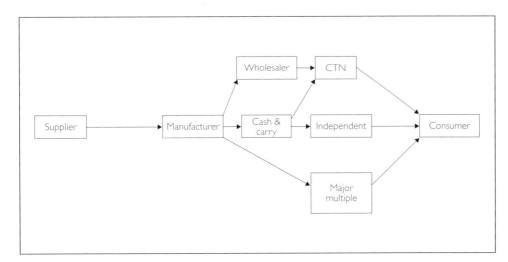

**FIGURE 10.6**

**Current market map for the drinks market**

## Future drinks market

The first stage of modelling future developments in the drinks market was to consider the likely changes to current routes to consumers. The following trends were considered to be probable:

- growth in the overall size of the 'drinks' market

- a decline in the number of independent grocers, leading to a decline in the number of wholesalers

- an increase in sales through garage forecourts, particularly those partnering with supermarkets

- an increase in demand for home delivery, particularly for products consumed in large quantities, such as mineral water

- an increase in the diversity of food services (for example, juice bars)

- an increase in the demand for combinations of stimulant soft drinks and alcoholic drinks

- an increase in home shopping.

The trends most relevant to e-business were then examined in more detail. The findings are summarized below.

## Home shopping

The uptake of home shopping is dependent upon the co-ordination of purchase and delivery. It is likely to be most successful where a complete product set can be offered. Sales of single, low-value products are unlikely because they require too much effort in terms of ordering from many different sites and receiving multiple deliveries. Delivery costs are also higher, reducing any cost savings that home shopping has to offer.

*The uptake of home shopping is dependent upon the co-ordination of purchase and delivery.*

Where a complete product set can be offered to customers in a convenient and cost effective way, fulfilment of the order must be achieved at minimal inconvenience to the shopper. For this reason, a range of delivery mechanisms needs to be explored to assess their acceptance and effectiveness. Possible mechanisms include:

- collecting packages of goods from the store in a 'drive through' manner

- delivery of orders to the place of work

- collection points in garage forecourts or secure facilities at home.

## Information services and marketing

Customer intimacy will be key to success in the future soft drinks market, so direct marketing (whether online or offline) will need to be a core competence of manufacturers.

Customers will expect mass market products to be widely available (both online and offline). Product ubiquity will need to be accompanied by personalized interaction to reduce the effort and increase the perceived benefits to the customer. Only where the customer has a specialized need will he or she be prepared to invest effort in searching for products and determining product availability.

To achieve product ubiquity online and to provide a wide product range, infomediaries are likely to emerge, as shown in Figure 10.7. Manufacturers are only likely to succeed in acting as focused infomediaries where they have very strong brands. Manufacturers could, however, collaborate with non-competing businesses (for example, drinks and sports manufacturers) to develop communities of interest.

Highly specific health and fitness portals, or 'vortals' ('vertical portals', serving particular markets) are likely to be influential and will be used for advertising, or disseminating information about, nutritional products, pointing the consumer in the direction of the manufacturer for further information and re-inforcement of the brand message, or online retail sites to place orders. These portals will gain from the provision of added-value information services, such as the 'online sports coach' or 'online dietician'. The consumer may also view a manufacturer's website directly, gaining the URL from offline sources such as packaging.

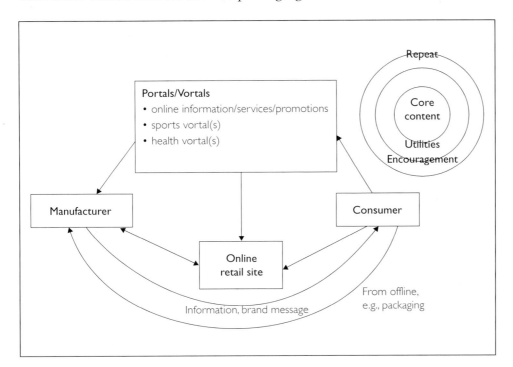

**FIGURE 10.7**

**Home shopping: information services and marketing**

## Business to business

There will be moves by both manufacturers and retailers to increase front-end and back-end collaboration within the supply chain. Who takes control of systems for information sharing will vary between different categories of retailer, with consequences for the style of system and the nature of the relationship (*see* Figure 10.8). A retailer-owned system, for example, might support the comparison of substitute offerings, whilst a manufacturer-owned system might hope to make purchasing from one manufacturer more convenient than purchasing from another. The technical sophistication of the retailer will also make it more likely that the retailer would control system-enabled relationships.

The number of manufacturers *versus* the number of buyers will also affect the distribution of power within the market. So, within the fragmented independents and CTN (confectioners, tobacconists and newsagents) cases,

*The number of manufacturers versus the number of buyers will also affect the distribution of power within the market.*

where there are large numbers of each, manufacturers have the opportunity – and the threat – of new online marketplaces, which match the large number of buyers to the large number of sellers. Wholesalers could potentially provide such marketplaces, utilizing their distribution networks as key strengths and re-inforcing them with hi-tech warehousing, which could also support home shopping.

**FIGURE 10.8**

**Soft drinks: Future manufacturer/retailer relationships**

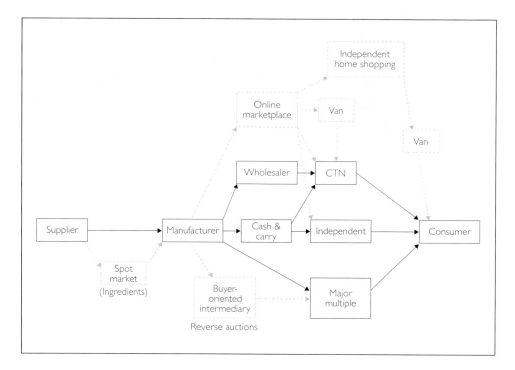

In the cases of major multiples and food services, though, where retailers are relatively few, the relationship is likely to take the form of Internet-based 'EDI' style systems, which support electronic ordering, stock enquiry and so on in a one-to-one relationship between retailer and manufacturer. The influence of these major purchasers leads to these systems being described as 'buyer-oriented' in Figure 10.8. Vending may be made more efficient through remote monitoring, leading to efficient replenishment and electronic payment. Added-value information could be provided to consumers at the machine.

# Worksheets for strategy tools

Worksheets for some of the major tools discussed in the report have been developed and are included here. Companies can use the worksheets to guide their use of the strategy development tools. Ideally, the worksheets should be completed in a workshop style meeting with the key stakeholders in the e-commerce project present. This ensures that a range of ideas and approaches are captured and that commitment to the resulting strategy can be assured from all relevant stakeholders.

# INTERNAL COMPETENCE DIMENSIONS

(This tool is *not* specifically concerned with e-commerce, but it is an essential starting point for later diagnostic tools)

**Customer intimacy**
Targeting markets precisely and tailoring products and service to the needs of specific customer groups, exceeding expectations and building loyalty

**Operational excellence**
Enabling products and services to be obtained reliably, easily and cost-effectively by customers, implying focus on business processes to outperform others, delivering low costs and consistent customer satisfaction

Customer intimacy

Prosperity

Success

Survival

Operational excellence

Product leadership

**Product leadership**
Continuing product innovation which meets customer needs. This implies not only creativity in developing new products and enhancing existing ones, but also astute market knowledge to ensure they sell

1. Score your company out of 10 on your current position against each of these three dimensions and join the lines up.

N.B.
- Score yourself 1–3 if you are currently below the minimum level required in your market
- Score yourself 4–6 if you are currently as good as the average in your sector
- Score yourself 7–10 if you currently exceed the average in your sector.

2. Score your company out of 10 on the position you would need to attain in, say, three years' time against each of their dimensions in order to ensure your continuing prosperity.

3. On a separate sheet, list some of the main strategies you will need to implement to achieve the desired positions. These will be useful for completing the next diagnostic exercises.

# RIVALRY AMONGST EXISTING/POTENTIAL COMPETITORS

| *How can/will e-commerce change the basis of competition?* | | Where does the company stand? | | |
| --- | --- | --- | --- | --- |
| | | Opportunities | | Threats |
| | | *Cost reduction* | *Customer value creating* | |
| 1. Threat of new entrants<br>*How can e-commerce build barriers to entry?* | (a) Market share/size/brand/service<br>(b) Leverage physical assets<br>(c) Provide dominant exchanges<br>(d) Cost/price<br>(e) Remote delivery of bitware<br>(f) Others | | | |
| 2. Bargaining power of suppliers<br>*How will e-commerce change the balance of power and relationships with suppliers?* | (a) e-Commerce enabled forward integration or disintermediation<br>(b) Lock-in<br>(c) Others | | | |
| 3. Bargaining power of buyers<br>*How can e-commerce build in switching costs or change customer relationships?* | (a) Price transparency<br>(b) Systems integration<br>(c) Aggregation of demand<br>(d) Others | | | |
| 4. Threat of substitute products/services<br>*Will e-commerce generate new ways of satisfying customer needs?* | (a) Remote delivery of bitware<br>(b) Others | | | |

## I. Current position

Locate your organization on each of the Six Is. Mark your location on the diagram below.
Use the notes on the next page to prompt you if you wish.

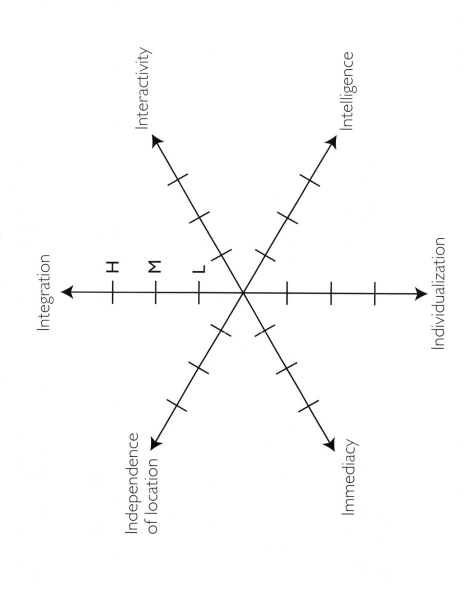

# NOTES ON THE SIX IS

### Integration of customer data

Do you have detailed knowledge of individual customers, influencers or consumers?

Do you share this knowledge across all customer-facing parts of the business?

### Interactivity

Do you use interactive media to allow your customers to communicate with you?

Do you listen to what they say and respond appropriately in a continuing dialogue?

### Independence of location

Do you exploit remote media such as mail, the telephone and the Internet to communicate with customers in a cost-effective manner wherever they are?

Do you exploit any opportunities to deliver information-based products and services electronically?

### Individualization

Do you use your customer knowledge to tailor products and services to the needs of particular individuals or segments?

Do you tailor all your communications to the characteristics of the recipients?

### Intelligence

Do you inform your marketing strategy with intelligence gleaned from your operational systems at the customer interface? (For example, through analysis of customer needs, segmentation, prioritizing segments according to customer lifetime value, etc.)

### Immediacy

Do you allow customers to contact you, learn about your products, match them to their needs, price them and order them whenever they want to, and using the minimum amount of their time?

Do you deliver the product/service and any post-sales service in as timely a manner as possible?

**THE E-MARKETING MIX (CONT)**

## 2. Future opportunities

Fill in the form below to indicate how e-commerce might improve the position of competitors on the Six Is, and how you might be able to exploit e-commerce yourselves.

| | Threats | e-Opportunities | |
| --- | --- | --- | --- |
| | | Cost reduction | Customer value creating |
| 1. Integration | | | |
| 2. Interactivity | | | |
| 3. Intelligence | | | |
| 4. Individualization | | | |
| 5. Immediacy | | | |
| 6. Independence of location | | | |

## FUTURE MARKET MAP

1. Having drawn the current market map, identify those points (junctions) where actual decisions are made about what is bought by the ultimate consumer/user and the percentage of total value/volume thus decided at each junction. In some cases, this point will be the ultimate consumer. In others, it may be a distributor or other influencer, such as an architect who, although not buying, say, radiators, decides for a builder what radiators should be bought.

2. Now do a buying factors analysis for each of these junctions, as follows.

(a) Name of decision-making junction, or segment

(b) List the most important buying factors considered by the members of this junction or segment

| | |
|---|---|
| 1 | |
| 2 | |
| 3 | |
| 4 | |
| 5 | |

(c) State the relative importance of each of these factors to the buyers. Score out of 100.

| |
|---|
| |
| |
| |
| |
| Total 100 |

3. Using your earlier analysis, in what ways can/will these needs be better met by e-commerce?

4. Now redraw the market map as it will be in, say, three to five years' time, given your knowledge about likely developments in the market, such as:
- new entrants
- new channels
- industry consolidation
- etc.

Cost reduction

| | |
|---|---|
| 1 | |
| 2 | |
| 3 | |
| 4 | |
| 5 | |

Value creation

| |
|---|
| |
| |
| |
| |

5. e-Opportunities
Draw up a list of opportunities for your organization.

# INFORMATION FLOWS AND THE CHANNEL MIX

1. For *each* major decision-making junction, now consider how information is obtained, leading to the purchase they make.

The following chart indicates the major steps in any purchase process (as column headings). Against each step, indicate where the relevant information is obtained by the decision maker. Thus, in each vertical column, what percentage of this task is currently completed using this medium?

|  | Initiate dialogue | Exchange information | Negotiate/tailor | Commit | Exchange value |
|---|---|---|---|---|---|
| Offline advertising (TV, press etc) |  |  |  |  |  |
| Direct mail |  |  |  |  |  |
| Sales force/face-to-face contact |  |  |  |  |  |
| Telephone |  |  |  |  |  |
| e-Commerce |  |  |  |  |  |
| Other (state:) |  |  |  |  |  |

3. Re-assess the percentages in these columns in, say, three to five years' time, taking account of e-commerce.

4. e-Opportunities
Take the e-commerce row and list the e-commerce communication opportunities for your organization.

| Cost reduction | | Value creation |
|---|---|---|
| 1 |  |  |
| 2 |  |  |
| 3 |  |  |
| 4 |  |  |
| 5 |  |  |

# INTERNAL VALUE CHAIN

Only for organizations for whom key accounts are of major significance. For each key account, list ways in which you can use e-commerce to improve the key account's value chain, by reducing their costs or creating value for their customers.

| | Reducing cost | Creating value |
|---|---|---|
| Infrastructure<br>– legal, accounting, financial management | | |
| Human resource management<br>– personnel, pay, recruitment, training, manpower planning, etc. | | |
| Product and technology development<br>– product and process design, production engineering, market testing, R&D, etc. | | |
| Procurement<br>– supplier management, funding, subcontracting, specification | | |

| | Inbound logistics<br>e.g., quality control receiving raw material control etc. | Operations<br>e.g., manufacturing packaging production control quality control maintenance etc. | Outbound logistics<br>e.g., finishing goods order handling despatch delivery invoicing etc. | Sales and marketing<br>e.g., customer mgmt order taking promotion sales analysis market research etc. | Servicing<br>e.g., warranty maintenance education/ training upgrade etc. |
|---|---|---|---|---|---|
| Reducing costs | | | | | |
| Creating value | | | | | |

# References

Berthon, P., Lane, N., Pitt, L. and Watson, R.T. (1996) 'Marketing communications and the world wide web', *Business Horizons*, September–October, pp 24–32.

Berthon, P., Lane, N., Pitt, L. and Watson, R.T. (1998) 'The world wide web as an industrial marketing communication tool: Models for the identification and assessment of opportunities'.

Boston Consulting Group (1999) *The Future of On-line Retailing*, USA.

Cash, J.I. (1988) 'Inter-organizational systems: an information society, opportunity or threat?', *The Information Society*, Vol. 3, No. 3.

Chambers, J. (2000) *Net Ready: Strategies for Success in the E-conomy*, New York: McGraw-Hill.

Daniel, E. (1998) 'On-line Banking: Winning the Majority', *Journal of Financial Services Marketing*, Vol. 2, No. 3, 259–270.

Hartman, A. and Sifonis, J. (2000) *Net Ready: Strategies for Success in the New Economy*, New York: McGraw-Hill.

IDC (2000) e-commerce market forecasts available at www.nua.ie/surveys.

Kalakota, R. and Whinston, A. (1998) *Electronic Commerce: A Manager's Guide*, USA: Addison Wesley.

Kim, W.C. and Mauborgne, R. (1999) 'Creating new market space', *Harvard Business Review*, January–February, 83–93.

Kotler, P. (1994) *Marketing management: analysis, planning, implementation and control*. Englewood Cliffs, NJ: Prentice Hall.

McDonald, M.H.B. and Wilson, H.N. (1999a) 'E-marketing: improving marketing effectiveness in a digital world', Financial Times Prentice Hall, Pearson Education Ltd, London.

McDonald, M.H.B. and Wilson, H.N. (1999b) 'Exploiting technique interrelationships: a model of strategic marketing planning', *Journal of Euro-Marketing*, 7(3), 1–26.

McDonald, M.H.B. and Dunbar, I. (1998) *Market Segmentation: How to do it, How to profit from it*, Basingstoke: Macmillan.

Neeley, Andrew (1999) *Measurement Design Record Sheet*, Cranfield School of Management.

Ostlund, L.E. (1974) 'Perceived Innovation Attributes as Predictors of Innovativeness', *Journal of Consumer Research*, Vol. 1, No. 2, 23–29.

Porter, M.E. (1984) *Competitive Advantage*, NY: Free Press.

Rayport, J.F. and Sviokla, J.J. (1995) 'Exploiting the Virtual Value Chain', *Harvard Business Review*, November/December.

Rogers, E. (1962) *The Diffusion of Innovations*. NY: Free Press.

Satbell, C.B. and Fjeldstad, O.D. (1998) 'Configuring Value for Competitive Advantage: On Chains, Shops and Networks', *Strategic Management Journal*, Vol. 19, 413–437.

Symonds, M. (1999) 'The net imperative: a survey of business and the Internet'. *The Economist*, 26 June.

Travis, A. (1999) 'Poll points to lift off for Internet', *The Guardian*, 11 January.

Treacy, M. and Wiersema, F. (1993) 'Customer Intimacy and Other Value Disciplines', *Harvard Business Review*, January/February.

Ward, J. (2000) 'Value chain analysis and electronic commerce – an overview', Paper for *Effective Strategies for Electronic Commerce* ISRC Research Project. Cranfield School of Management.

Ward, J. and Griffiths, P. (1996) *Strategic Planning for Information Systems*. Chichester: Wiley.

Ward, J. and Murray, P. (2000) 'Benefits Management Best Practice Guidelines', Cranfield School of Management.